Baby James

A Legacy of Love and Family Courage

Baby James

A LEGACY OF LOVE AND FAMILY COURAGE

Thomas and Jayne Miller

**Afterword: A Physician's Perspective
by Leonard L. Bailey, M.D.**

1817

Harper & Row, Publishers, San Francisco
Cambridge, Hagerstown, New York, Philadelphia, Washington
London, Mexico City, São Paulo, Singapore, Sydney

FIRST EDITION

Library of Congress Cataloging-in-Publication Data

Miller, Thomas, 1945–
    Baby James : a legacy of love and family courage / Thomas and Jayne Miller ; afterword, A physician's perspective by Leonard L. Bailey.
        p.   cm.
    ISBN 0-06-250584-X
    1. Miller, Nicholas Lawrence, 1985–1986 —Health.   2. Heart—Transplantation—Patients—California—Biography.
    3. Transplantation of organs, tissues, etc. in children—California—Biography.   I. Miller, Jayne.   II. Title.
    RD598.M48M55 1988
    362.1'97412'0092—dc19
    [B]   87-46221
                                                                  CIP

---

88 89 90 91 92 HC 10 9 8 7 6 5 4 3 2 1

For Nicholas
who gave such joy

Contents

THE BEGINNING

This is the story of a little boy, a mom, and a dad—a story of how we came together, of our triumph over tragedy, and of the love we've shared in the sight of God.

This is also the story of three miracles. The first miracle was the two of us—Tom and Jayne—meeting and choosing to spend the rest of our lives together. The second was Nicholas' surviving when no one had any business surviving. The third was Nicholas' receiving his new heart.

Though it could be argued that the first and last are miracles only in our own minds, the second is certifiable. The chief doctor at Stanford Hospital's neonatal Intensive Care Nursery told us so.

❦

Because we parented Nicholas together, we—Tom, Nicholas' dad, and Jayne, Nicholas' mom—have chosen to tell the story of our son together *as a team*. Rather than emphasize Jayne's thoughts or Tom's thoughts, we've highlighted our "coupleness" throughout our experiences by writing from our shared point of view. When, at times, an action or thought is specific or special to one or the other, we do our best to make that clear. In truth, our story is by each of us and both of us.

When Nicholas came into this world, he was a little pioneer. At his appearance, life became something altogether special for us all, sometimes bone-chilling, more often joyous, always the quintessence of love. Certainly there were pain and happiness—both by the cornucopiaful—and unexpected turns enough for many lifetimes. Tom sometimes reflects on our experiences and, in his more expansive moods, likens them to adventures. But scenes from

Indiana Jones and old Tarzan movies didn't spring to mind back when we were confronted with a well-meaning doctor who told us that our eight-day-old baby was dying and she didn't know why. All there was in the world that day was our love for our son, and a fear that shook us to our very souls.

≈§

We named our son Nicholas Lawrence. *Nicholas* was chosen for Jayne's maternal grandfather, an influential man in the paper industry during the middle of this century. Jayne was ten when he died, and her memories of him are vivid and special. *Lawrence* was after T. E. Lawrence—Lawrence of Arabia. The Academy Award–winning picture about him is Tom's favorite movie. So Nicholas was named after a paper magnate and a true-to-life adventure hero. At some point after we were firmly committed to this name, but long before he was born, we looked up the derivations and meanings of *Nicholas Lawrence* in a baby name book. What we learned pleased us; we'd happened upon a name bursting with strength and grand hope. Soon enough, though, we would learn that our son's name was appropriate far beyond our intentions.

When our little pioneer came frighteningly close to a precipice, as he so often did, we always tried to keep uppermost in our minds the certainty of God's plan for us. We saw clearly from the start that, regardless of how the "adventure" ended, without Nicholas, we would not have known the experience of parenting, and without us, Nicholas would not have known the love of family. Every minute we tried to fortify these feelings.

That Nicholas came into our lives at all is, in our view, an underscoring of God's presence in the world. It is our firm belief that it was God's plan that the three of us be brought together. This is our story.

OUR STORY

Chapter One

Valentine's Day 1985 raced to a close. Midnight fast approached. We'd put down our books and turned off the light; we lay in bed snuggled close. Then, as we do every night, we offered a prayer before drifting off to sleep. This night's prayer, though, sprang from a special place in our hearts. Usually we thanked God for one another, then asked for His guidance.

This night we also asked for a "sign" about Gabriel, a twelve-and-a-half-month-old boy from Tacoma, Washington. His mother had contacted us two weeks earlier to discuss adoption. We were excited by this possibility, but we had concerns. We anxiously wanted to adopt and start our family, but our mental image of our first child was of a newborn infant. Besides, not only would the boy have the difficult adjustment of suddenly having new parents and a new environment, he'd also be given a new name. Our first son's name had been chosen seven years before, within weeks of our engagement. In our minds' eye, our first boy was Nicholas Lawrence. Thus we prayed for a sign from the Lord to help answer the question paramount in our minds: Were we meant to welcome the blond, curly-haired little Gabriel into our family? Then we dropped off to sleep.

Tom got out of bed at three-thirty—not his normal wake-up time by any means—in order to arrive at his Silicon Valley job by five. It was a Friday, and the next day he'd start a week's vacation at home, while Jayne continued to work. He needed to start early that day to meet a deadline and wrap up loose ends so that he could go home that evening without taking the office with him.

A full nine days to relax in our "country" log house set in a mossy glen on the San Francisco Peninsula—and to work on his mystery novel! Tom's biggest frustration at that point in his life was that his job took so much time and energy that he had little left over for writing. Perhaps he could even finish the first draft! He looked forward to this vacation as never before.

Just before he left the house, he stood at Jayne's bedside, gazing down at her quiet figure. He loved looking at her face when she slept. With her short light-brown hair, and the blanket pulled up to her chin, the little girl came out in her. He whispered, "I love you," and brushed a curl off her forehead. He nearly always did this, whether the curl needed brushing or not. As he did so, he offered a silent prayer: *Lord, please let Jayne's and my love continue to grow with each passing day, and may our lives together be long so that we may fully enjoy the wonder of our life together.* At four-forty he drove off.

RRRING! Jayne was jolted awake. It was nearly pitch black in the house. The bedroom phone rang again. By the blue glow of the digital alarm clock on Tom's side of the bed, her worst fear was confirmed: it was only five-twenty. *Tom must have been in an accident!* Her pulse raced as she jumped out of bed and answered the phone. A woman's formal voice at the other end said, "Mrs. Miller, this is District Hospital—"

Her heart pounded in terror. Her thoughts rushed in a pleading litany, *Please, let him be alive. Oh, Lord, please, just let him be alive!*

"—Labor and Delivery calling," the voice concluded.

Her fear instantly vanished. This wasn't a call of doom. Not only was Tom okay, but perhaps a long-cherished dream had come true. Jayne held her breath.

"You have a son. He was born at 5:08 A.M. His parents read the letter you'd written explaining why you wanted to adopt, and they want you to have him. He's beautiful." The nurse then asked Jayne to write down a few important things that we needed to bring along to the hospital. "Be sure you have identification—a driver's license will do. Remember, you'll need to go to the Medical Records department; bring the guardianship papers your attorney has provided you with, and your attorney's name and phone number. . . ."

Jayne, who excused herself when the caller paused for breath, ran all around the house looking for a pen or pencil, only to return to the phone breathless and empty-handed. There, right beside the phone, were a pen and notepad! In a few minutes, having made the required notes, she rang off.

In the meantime, Tom, his sleeves rolled up and his tie loosened, intently plowed through the manuscripts, typesetting orders, and print request forms that he worked with as editor/publications production coordinator for a laptop computer manufacturer. Taking a moment's respite, he leaned back in his chair, ran the fingers of one hand through the back of his thinning gray-brown hair, and rubbed his neck. As far as he could tell, he was the only person on the administrative floor. He'd needed to turn on the lights in order to find his way to his desk. Now he heard a low chime whisper through the building, indicating an incoming phone call on the main number. He picked up his receiver and dialed the code that allowed him to answer the call.

"Tom speaking," he said.

"Tommy, we have a son!" Jayne exploded. "District Hospital just called. They have a baby for us, a little boy. We finally have our little Nicholas!"

Forty minutes later, at 6:05 A.M., we saw Nicholas Lawrence Miller for the first time: tiny, perfectly formed, less than an hour old, he slept bundled in a blue-yellow-and-white plaid receiving blanket in a clear plastic hospital bassinet on the other side of the observation window.

"My goodness, Jayne, look! He has my high forehead." As Tom spoke, he could see himself grinning in the window reflection.

"And my coloring." Jayne was holding her arm out, comparing her son's skin tones with her own. "How could he be so much like us?"

We looked at one another, wide-eyed, and shook our heads in wonder. To think that this little boy was *our* son! We could hardly believe it. Yet not only was Nicholas Lawrence truly in front of us then and there in flesh and blood, but he proved more beautiful, more perfectly formed than we had ever dared to imagine. He was real—the culmination of shared hopes and dreams that went back seven years.

Standing outside that window—or were we floating?—holding each other tightly, almost afraid to let go, we bonded with Nicholas. It was then, during those first few minutes, that he became irrevocably and forever part of our family. All else that followed—all of our decisions, actions, and knee-jerk responses— were in a very real sense decided right then and there. Without our even being conscious of it, a boundless, unalterable parental love and sense of responsibility sprang into being.

Yes, of course we knew that he wasn't *officially* ours yet, that his birthmother could change her mind at any time in the next six months and take him away from us, but in our hearts he'd become *our* child. He wasn't just a baby we happened to be adopting. Nicholas was clearly and simply our son from those first moments we gazed at him. We could no more have given him up than we could a biological child—regardless of what the future held. It was simply unthinkable.

Jayne said, "Oh, Tom, I hope he never has to go to war." An irrational statement from an ecstatic new mom. Little did we know of the battles the three of us would soon be fighting.

We remained outside the nursery window for two hours, watching nurses come in, check his vitals, and fuss around him. Bursting with pride, we drank in every detail that we could of this little boy.

From the start, our dealings with the hospital were different than other parents would have expected. Jayne was a respiratory therapist on staff there—had been for seven years. She had worked to save lives beside many of the doctors and nurses. She was highly experienced in critical care situations, and medical terminology was second nature to her. As a result, the hospital staff spoke to Jayne comfortably, more as a colleague than as a first-time mother.

One of the nurses, for instance, came out of the birthmother's room too excited to remember that she hadn't any business discussing details with us. "Oh, Jayne," she said, "you should see the father. He's at least six-foot-five, and very handsome! He must be a basketball player."

Another nurse reported that Nicholas' mother was "attractive in an average sort of way" and that she had a shy smile and a deep dimple in her chin.

And so it went. As the nurses came out one by one from the nursery to visit with us, we slowly learned how Nicholas had entered our lives.

Beth, a tall, soft-spoken nurse whom Jayne didn't know because they worked opposite shifts, had reported to work in Labor and Delivery at eleven the previous evening. It looked to be a quiet night—there weren't any moms in labor—so she and Gussey, the other nurse on duty, decided to tidy up the nursing station. They bustled around the desk for a while; then they tackled the bulletin board.

"Gussey, why don't you take down that thank-you note with the pictures," Beth said.

"Oh no, Beth, we can't take that down. That's not a thank-you note. That's a letter from a woman who works here in Respiratory and her husband. They're trying to adopt a baby."

They were discussing one of the 1,600 adoption search letters we had sent all over the country to doctors, guidance counselors, and hospitals. In them we explained who we were and why we wanted to adopt.

Beth, who had never read our posted letter, who had assumed for fourteen months that it was a thank-you note from a prior patient, was intrigued. She took down the letter and read it.

Hello—
We want very much to adopt a child. Our life together is very full and blessed; however, we really miss having a child to share it with. We not only have love and a warm home to share, we feel we are good at enriching little lives. . . .

Beth felt touched as she read through it. She studied our picture and that of our log home and announced to Gussey, "We have to try to help these people. Someday soon we'll find them a baby."

What we couldn't explain in the short space of a letter was our sense of *incompleteness*, our deep frustration, wanting to share the love we could feel ourselves overflowing with, but not having a child we could share it with. We knew in our souls that we both had much to offer a child. Our talents and abilities, our perspectives on life and God, our dreams, and our proven child-care aptitude all convinced us that we would be good parents—if only we had a chance!

Jayne, as an oldest child, had participated actively in the care of three younger sisters and a brother. In high school, she enjoyed babysitting and teaching religious education classes so much that she chose to work her way through college as a live-in nanny. In fact, she still heard from many of her charges as they grew up, graduated from high school and college, married, and had their own children.

Tom's little brother, Rodger, came into the world at the same time their parents' divorce became final. At the age of twelve, Tom, whose older brother had left home to join the Marine Corps, found himself the only grown male in the house, and he became devoted to his little brother and helped his mom bring him up. Tom spent much of his free time with Rodger, steadily teaching him how to read the big letters in newspaper headlines, in movie advertisements, and on record album covers. As a result, Rodger could read by the age of three.

But none of this could be put in the letter.

At four-fifteen that morning, Nicholas' birthmother and birthfather had arrived at District Hospital. She was in hard labor; delivery was imminent. The mother had received no prenatal care and did not have a physician, so the doctor on call was notified immediately. As Beth was prepping her for delivery, the birthmother said, "We're not going to keep this baby. It's being given up for adoption. We don't want to see it. Please wrap it as soon as it's born and take it to the nursery." Beth agreed and asked for the name of the agency to call. The woman responded, "I made an appointment for later today with the County Child Services Agency. Just call them. They can tell you what to do next."

But Beth remembered our letter and said, "Since you haven't relinquished your baby to the agency, perhaps you would consider reading a letter we have here from one of our employees and her husband." The birthparents agreed to read the letter together. Afterwards they both said, "Let them have our baby." They also said that because they'd seen our photograph, they didn't need to meet us.

The doctor arrived moments later and counseled the couple about the seriousness of their decision. "Though by California law you'll have six months to reconsider and take your baby back," he said, "you should be absolutely sure that this adoption is what you want. Remember that three other lives will be affected—your child's and his adoptive parents'. It's cruel to give a child up now and take him back later on."

The birthparents both assured the doctor that they were firm in their resolve not to raise the child. Soon after, at 5:08 A.M., after only slightly more than an hour of labor, the woman delivered a boy.

At birth Nicholas weighed 7 pounds, 14 ounces, and was 20.5 inches long. He had Apgar newborn evaluation scores of 9 and 10 (out of a possible 10), which meant that he appeared alert and healthy. He had a lusty cry, olive coloring, strong muscle tone, and a great predilection to wiggle!

Since we never did meet the birthparents, all we learned of them—other than the few bits we heard from the nurses—was what they included in their medical history profile: mainly that they came from French, Dutch, and English backgrounds and that they were both in good health.

Word spread quickly that Jayne and Tom Miller had finally found a baby to adopt. Many in the hospital knew of our seemingly endless fourteen-month national search effort and rushed up to the third floor to congratulate us. The nurse manager for Perinatal Services arrived at work at eight and right away came to the observation window.

"Come with me," she said. "I bet you'd like to hold your baby now." She guided us into the "scrub room" and helped us slip yellow cloth gowns over our clothes.

Nicholas was exactly three hours old when Jayne held her son for the first time. He was very pink and had lots of straight dark hair and a perfectly formed "cupid's bow" upper lip.

She looked from the tiny warm bundle in her arms to Tom, who was lost in a loving gaze. After all, he'd never seen his wife and son together before!

Jayne smiled. "You know, Tom, I've held many babies before," she said, "but I'm marveling at how *special* this little one feels."

Tom blinked several times as his eyes grew misty. "Well, we've been bonding for three hours," he said. "They say that's how it happens. His life is now in our hands."

Soon after, Tom, feeling very much a daddy, gently took Nicholas from Jayne's arms. Unable to stop grinning, he looked down into the face of the sleeping little boy who was now totally dependent on us, and he was filled with a sense of joyous responsibility. He brushed our son's tiny cheeks, nose, and forehead with his fingertips. It was so hard to believe that just hours before, this little person had been only a bright spark in our dreams and had seemed, more often than not, hopelessly remote. Now he was real and in our arms, and it was as though Nicholas Lawrence had always been ours!

"I just know he'll be a senator someday," Tom said.

"But it'll be okay if he's not," Jayne responded. "He could be a bus driver or a farmer or anything else he wanted to be."

Tom frowned as a thought struck him. "Do you realize that by the time he grows up, traveling to the moon and Mars could be common?"

Jayne laughed at the mental picture. "Can you imagine it? When he gets married, he'll announce that he and his bride are going to *honeymoon* on the *moon*!"

"But you know," Tom went on excitedly, taking his train of thought even further, "if he becomes a senator, he could even become president of the solar system!"

Jayne shook her head and chuckled at Tom's imaginative meanderings. "Settle down, darling. Let's get him out of diapers first."

We grinned at one another and were filled with the happiness that only a dream come true can bring. So many dreams had been realized with Nicholas' birth . . . and we had so much to talk about.

A nurse brought in a bottle, and Tom returned Nicholas to Jayne's arms for his first feeding. Our son quickly began sucking and took his first ounce of formula like a champ. Jayne held him up to burp him and discovered the cuddler in him. He felt so cozy nestled on her shoulder.

The entire morning slipped by before Tom, bubbling over with excitement, dashed back to the office to finish his work. His co-workers were thunderstruck and happy that he was "suddenly" a father. Then, after setting a record for dispatching mounds of paperwork, he rushed back.

Freshly gowned and scrubbed, he joyfully rejoined Jayne, who was in the midst of a conversation with George, one of her co-workers. "Just think," George was saying, looking over the top of half-rim glasses, "you'll get to watch Nicholas grow up—first giggles, first words, first steps." He pumped Tom's hand. "Before you know it, he'll be off to his first day at school."

We all grinned happily, imagining these milestones and so many others that we hoped to share with Nicholas. Our country garden would soon be in bloom. The hundreds of spring bulbs we'd planted the previous fall had begun to poke through the earth. It was exciting to think of the extravaganza of color we'd soon share with our son.

And our cat, Kipling! He'd no longer be our substitute child. How would he cope with the exploring hands of an infant and toddler?

Then we realized, as most new parents do, that we were ahead of ourselves. Teaching the colors of flowers and cat etiquette would come in time, as would park adventures, trips to the library, and gleeful explorations. The true joy of first-time parenting would be in *watching and sharing:* watching Nicholas change each day and grow and become the person he was meant to be, and sharing ourselves and our experiences with him, teaching him and letting him teach us the joy of life and love and family.

Most of all, we focused on the breathtaking thought that this little boy felt so much like our son already. The fact that he had birthparents other than us seemed remote, a mere technicality.

Was this because we'd wanted a child for so very long, or because he looked so much like us? Would we have felt this way about any child who came into our lives? Or was this little boy somehow special . . . somehow *meant* for us? All we knew for sure was that the lives of Nicholas and his new mom and dad were irrevocably linked from those moments on; somehow we could sense the Lord's plan unfolding, and we were grateful beyond words that God had chosen to bring him into our lives.

Meanwhile Dr. Laurie Rubenstein came in to examine Nicholas. We had spoken to her months before about our adoption hopes. Now, with only one phone call from us, she made good on her months-earlier promise to be our child's pediatrician.

Radiantly blond and statuesque, she made quite a picture as she exclaimed, "Hey, guys, he's doing *really* well!" Laurie *always* communicated in exclamations because she was always *terrifically* excited by her little patients. "Look how *beautiful* he is!"

It occurred to Tom to ask a question, but all he could get out of his mouth was, "When—?" Typical of Laurie, she was ten steps ahead.

"Oh, I'll be back at five to circumcise him. Then my husband and I are leaving for a week in Mexico. The doctor covering for me, who's terrific, will be available should any questions arise."

But before Laurie left, Jayne needed some basic questions answered: "What formula do you recommend? How often should we feed him?" After talking about support systems and feeding schedules, and firming up an appointment for a week from Monday, Laurie said, "And you can take Nicholas home in the morning."

Although Jayne had expected this, Tom was surprised. "So soon? That's great! I guess times have changed."

"That's right. You guys will be a happy family of three at home hardly more than a day after his birth."

We spent the rest of the afternoon at the hospital, Nicholas in our arms most of the time. He gurgled and smiled, and we marveled aloud at each such "major accomplishment." At one point, we called our dear friends Mima and Daniel Horne, arranging for them to come by the hospital in the evening to meet Nicholas, and to help us celebrate our happiness by joining us for dinner. Earlier in the day, Jayne had made two quick calls—one to her parents, announcing that they had a new grandchild, and the other to Mima. It was just six in the morning then, but Jayne knew that Mima wouldn't mind being awakened with such grand news. Indeed, Mima, the mother of two young sons, squealed with delight. "Your adoption search is over! That's terrific. And you have a son. Wait till Spencer and Robin hear that 'Auntie Jayne' has a new baby."

While we were at the newborn-care class and bathing demonstration, the Hornes arrived and found their way to the observation window. They'd been making faces at Nicholas for several minutes when we caught them in the act. Daniel explained: "Oh, we were just getting acquainted, as it were."

We chatted with our friends outside the window for a while, then regowned and went back into the nursery to hug and kiss our little boy. Leaving Nicholas in the capable hands of the nurses, we joined Mima and Daniel and left for a Chinese restaurant. We had much to celebrate!

Chapter Two

This special night, our foursome sat at a table near a pint-sized replica of an Easter Island giant. The main dining room was a veritable paradise of colorfully spotlighted waterfalls, tiny bubbling streams, brilliant orchids, and native idols.

"Can you believe it?" Daniel exclaimed, smoothing down his thick mustache with two adept strokes. "You're parents!"

"Mr. Miller," Mima said to Tom with mock seriousness, "when you met Jayne, could you have believed that this day would someday happen?"

Tom looked first at Jayne, then from Mima's fresh, radiant face to Daniel's cherubic one. Mima and Daniel were both blond—a classic case of a married couple who had been together so long that they looked like brother and sister.

Before Tom could answer, Daniel broke in: "Tell us again how you two met. It's been nearly eight years since I heard the story." Daniel was referring to the first time the Hornes and the Millers had dined together in Jayne's apartment in Menlo Park, on the occasion of Mima and Daniel's seventh wedding anniversary—just two months after our engagement.

Tom always loved to tell this story; he was about to launch into it when the waiter made a sudden appearance. They quickly chose from the menu; then Tom began the tale.

"It was in April of 1978, and I was working for a San Francisco TV station. I'd been there eight years in several different positions. Jayne would say that I had my finger on the pulse of the station. Anyway, late one afternoon, when I was in the lobby taking a break and looking out the front window, this attractive lass strode down the sidewalk right up toward me—perfect posture she had, mind you. I opened the door for her and she asked me if I could get Tom for her, please. 'My name is Tom,' I said. 'Will I do?' "

"I was really impressed with how *bold* he was," Jayne broke in. "But I said, 'No, thank you. I was looking for Tom Wagner.' Then Tom—*this* Tom—tried to find the other Tom, who was a show director and the guy I was going out with at the time; but he was in the middle of doing a show, so we struck up a conversation."

"I don't remember everything we said," Tom continued, "but at some point I brought up my cat, Doyle. Jayne asked, 'After Doyle Drive [a notorious San Francisco street] or Sir Arthur Conan?' This was so amazing that I nearly fell over. Frankly, it's a very rare woman—indeed a rare person—who can talk knowledgeably about Arthur Conan Doyle." Tom smiled at Mima and Daniel, who knew they were among the elite—Daniel particularly, for he was a librarian. "From there we began to talk about Sherlock Holmes and eventually drifted into my philosophy of life. I said something like, 'My interests lean toward the infinite and the infinitesimal.' When she asked me to explain, I told her how I enjoyed meditating on both the enormity of the universe and the diminishing smallness that happens inside atoms. To which she again responded astutely, and I was blown away. In all my thirty-one years, I had never—repeat *never*—met a woman who could converse about these currents of thought within me."

"And for my part," Jayne said, "I was impressed by his chattering. (Little did I know what an introvert he really was.) From the first second, we hit it off as friends. But I was still going with the other Tom at the time."

"How did you meet the other Tom?" Mima asked.

"I have a priest friend who was host of a Saturday afternoon religious talk show, and he invited me to watch it being taped. I met the director, and we starting going out. But after I met *this* Tom and found out he wasn't seeing anyone, I wanted to set him up with one of my single friends. For five months I tried—"

"Without my knowing it!" Tom broke in.

"—but I kept asking the wrong people at the wrong times, and nothing ever came of it. Anyway, the other Tom and I eventually broke up. Then *this* Tom found out about it, and we had lunch."

The waiter appeared at this point with the appetizers, leaving behind bowls of clear won-ton soup and a lazy Susan with tiny barbequed ribs, crispy spring rolls, pot stickers, red cocktail sauce, and hot mustard.

"Which brings me to your original question, Mima," Tom said. "Sure, we've anticipated this day since our first date. In fact . . . hmmm, during that first lunch, I said some strange things—which only goes to prove that some of our strongest convictions can be just so much hot air given the right circumstances. For instance—it's hard to believe this really happened, but I assure you it's true—I told Jayne then that I was convinced that marriage was an outdated institution. I had no desire to get married; it was clear that marriage didn't work in today's society. Hadn't nearly all the marriages of my friends and family ended in divorce? I knew firsthand about the obsolescence of marriage.

"I also said that I'd always wanted my first child to be a girl—I guess because I had wanted a sister my whole life but had two brothers instead."

"My comment, then," Jayne giggled, "was what a terrible pressure to put on a wife. What if your first child was a boy? Can you imagine the poor woman's postpartum depression? She'd be devastated!"

"To which I replied that I was extremely adaptable—boy or girl, I would love the child completely."

Tom looked at his wife, sitting next to him in a big wicker fan-backed chair, and held out his hand. Jayne took it and they gazed at one another for a moment in silence.

"Well, three and a half weeks later, I was engaged," Tom went on, "and today I have a beautiful wife, a newborn son, and I'm the happiest man alive. There's got to be a moral there somewhere.

"To elaborate even further on your question, Mima," Tom continued, "our engagement was simply a reflection of our growing commitment to one another. It's as though we said, 'We recognize our potential as a dynamite couple. We're proud of our strengths and want to share them. And not only that, between the two of us, we'll have really great kids, and our family will be strong.' And as that sense of ourselves as a truly committed couple kept growing stronger, our desire to have a family also grew. Our first thoughts on children were that we'd have two of our own, then adopt a third. After all, the world is full of needy children. So the possibility of adopting was with us from the start. But it was only two years ago that we really started considering adoption for our first child as well."

"What made you decide then?" Daniel asked.

Jayne said, "Our three emotional miscarriages. You see, beginning months before our wedding, I had occasional bouts of hypertensive adrenal crisis (though at the time, nobody had a name to pin on the symptoms), and in 1981 I was hospitalized. In June 1982, I submitted to an evaluation at the University of California Medical Center in San Francisco. After four months of rigorous testing, it was determined that my body had a rare endocrine abnormality and wasn't able to produce a chemical called 17 hydroxylase, and that both my adrenals . . ."

Jayne had unconsciously shifted into "hospitalese" as she spoke to Mima, a nurse. To spare Daniel, Tom interrupted. "Daniel, what Jayne is trying to say is that because of the way her body reacts to other-than-normal stress, she probably can't carry a child to full term. Even if she could, she might be risking her health and the baby's. The hormonal changes of pregnancy are simply too much for her body to handle."

"So you decided to adopt when you finally got a diagnosis," Daniel said, methodically trying to pinpoint a time of decision.

"No," Tom said, "for a few months, we put the whole matter on psychological hold. Frankly, we were in a kind of shock. There was even a brief period when we discussed the possibility of *not* having children. We had a lot of other things to worry about, too. We were trying to get my new career in publishing off the ground, since I was spinning my wheels in a dead end at the TV station. We were also trying to save money to buy a home, so we were both working long hours. But after we had our final miscarriage, we began talking seriously about adoption again. Then Doyle died."

From the time Tom adopted Doyle, our gray tabby, as a kitten in 1976, he treated his cat just as though he were another person. But during Doyle's last three years, we were told over and again that, despite his healthy appearance, he had a serious, untreatable heart murmur.

"When Doyle died," Jayne said, "there was suddenly a void in our lives. Tom was distraught for days. I felt so helpless."

"Jayne comes from an immense family, you know," Tom said. "She has twenty-nine first cousins alone. So deaths and funerals have always been a part of her life. On the other hand, I had only my mom and two brothers. Nobody in my family had died. So Doyle's death was pretty rough on me."

"We both missed him terribly," Jayne said. "Within three days, we had decided that we had to adopt another kitten to fill the void. We found a four-month-old gray tabby who had a pronounced bump on his nose. Because it was Christmas time and Tom wouldn't think of naming a cat after anything except a Victorian author, we called him Dickens."

"After we had Dickens a few days, everything came together," Tom said, taking up the story. "I'll never forget it; it was a magical moment. Jayne and I had just crawled into bed and Dickens was curled up at the foot of the bed. 'You know,' I said, 'you and I have an awful lot of love to give. It's as if we're overflowing and need someone outside of ourselves to share it with.' We just looked at one another, and we *knew*. 'Should I start looking seriously into adopting?' Jayne asked. 'Yes,' I said, 'it's time.' Well, that's all Jayne needed. Give her a task, no matter how involved, as long as at its end is something she wants, and she's up to her elbows in it in nothing flat."

Just then several piping hot dishes were placed in the center of the table—shrimp in lobster sauce, lemon chicken, beef with broccoli, and fried rice. As we served ourselves and began to eat, Jayne described how we went about trying to adopt a baby.

Initially we made calls to the County Adoption Services Agency. The responses were discouraging, and we were told—only after all our paperwork was completed—that we could expect a five- to eight-year wait for a baby. This led us to investigate other options. Catholic Social Services warned us of a three- to five-year wait. We then began checking into private adoption. In January Jayne posted a note in the Labor and Delivery suite at District Hospital, where she worked. Then we met with an adoption counselor who specialized in private, or independent, adoption. "Tell everyone you know that you want to adopt a baby. Someday you'll meet someone who'll know someone who's planning to give up a baby, and before you know it, you'll be parents."

Then we sent out the search letter, which eventually generated a few leads, and we heard of another dozen through word of mouth. Unfortunately all the leads came through a friend of a friend of a friend. Though at first they gave us hope that we'd soon be successful, by the time we'd weeded through the maze of well-meaning friends and family who had elected themselves as buffers for the women themselves, it was too late. If the woman hadn't already had an abortion, then the child had been born and the mother had chosen to keep it.

The frustration began to mount. "Lord, will we ever become parents?" was our constant question and prayer. We continued to send letters and work with our attorney. We joined a support group composed both of other parents in our area who had adopted successfully and those who were still waiting.

Jayne began to fill our closets with baby things: a car seat, a layette, baby food, diapers, and a portable crib with sheets. We had the essentials. Should a call come suddenly, we were ready.

"Tom, though, ever the pragmatist, often laughed about this," Jayne teased. Then she mimicked his voice: 'Jayne, why are you gathering all this stuff? We don't even have a baby yet.' His favorite line during this period was, 'Show me a baby, and I'll believe in the baby.' My favorite retort was, 'They didn't name you Thomas for nothing. You sure are a doubter!' "

"So from Christmas of 1983 until this morning," Tom said, "we've simply been living our lives, following leads. The month before Doyle died, I'd gotten a job with a computer company. Then Dickens went out one day in April and never came back."

"You can imagine how upset we were," Jayne said.

Tom nodded. "A month went by, and I must have made a nuisance of myself in the neighborhood; every morning before I left for work and every evening when I came home, I'd walk down the country road that runs in front of our house calling Dickens' name. Eventually I gave up. I knew in my heart that he must have been run over. I decided then that there wouldn't be any more cats in our lives."

Jayne laughed. "His resolve lasted so long. By June he was scouring pet shelters looking for—you guessed it—another gray tabby, and eventually we found Kipling."

"But you know," Tom said, "when I look back on Doyle's dying and Dickens' entering our lives, I realize that if those things hadn't happened, there's a possibility we wouldn't be sitting here celebrating our good fortune today. It's as if Dickens had been sent to us to help us focus on what we really needed, and then he quietly departed. Kind of like the Lone Ranger."

Jayne looked at Tom and frowned. "Let's not get carried away."

"I can't help it," Tom responded. "It's a legitimate thought."

"Anyway, last month our attorney, aware of our frustration, suggested that we run classified ads in a number of out-of-state newspapers. Although adoption advertising isn't legal in some states, it can successfully bring babies together with people like ourselves. We placed an ad in a Washington state paper, and within days were contacted by a mom who wanted to give up her twelve-and-a-half-month-old son." We went on to explain that we were still in contact with her.

Mima said, "My goodness, wouldn't it be strange—in a wonderful sort of way—if after all your efforts, you suddenly had two little people enter your lives?"

Jayne smiled. "When it rains, it pours."

"What an incredible story," Daniel said. "I never realized it was so involved."

"And to think we just hit the high points!" Tom stretched his legs and laughed.

We ate quietly for a time, and then Mima said, "I just had a thought. Adopting Nicholas the way you are, not seeing or knowing his birthparents at all, you really don't have any preconceptions. It's as if you're beginning with a perfectly clean slate."

Jayne thought about this. "I see what you mean. If we'd gotten to know this woman—as is usually the case in private adoption—and we'd found out she had a temper, or was an alcoholic, or had freckles, or bad teeth, or *anything*, we'd probably wonder . . . and worry. Will the child need major dental work? Is he going to have a temper just like his mom? On and on."

"Yes, that's it. Even when you have your own children, you can't help having these kinds of thoughts. Will he have his uncle's mouth? Will he have his grandmother's disposition? Those are all questions I'd sooner have done without, believe me. But with Nicholas, you *can't* have them. He's a clean slate. You don't know *anything.*"

"Except that he'll probably be tall," Tom said.

"There is that." Mima laughed. "But trust me—having no preconceptions will be its own joy!"

"That may be true, Mima," Jayne said, "but I'm frankly a little disappointed by the birthparents' decision not to meet us. I think I would've liked to meet them—mainly to thank them and to be able to tell Nicholas a bit more about them when he gets older."

Mima responded with a knowing smile and said, "Oh, I can understand that, but someday you'll know what I'm saying."

Ever respectful of Mima's pearls of wisdom, Jayne answered, "Oh, I don't doubt it, Mima. I don't doubt it at all."

"Well, I imagine you two are anxious to get back to your son," Daniel said.

"You better believe it," Tom replied, signaling the waiter.

The bill was brought with four fortune cookies. Mima, Daniel, and Jayne broke theirs open, joking about the messages. At the same time, Tom opened his:

YOU ARE THE GUIDING STAR OF HIS EXISTENCE.

The shock of seeing those words struck him like a meteorite thundering through the ceiling. He stared at that little slip of paper as he'd never stared at anything before. The others noticed the change, and Jayne asked, "Tom, what's wrong?" He passed the fortune over. Mima and Daniel both said, "Well, what does it say?" Jayne read it aloud.

After a moment, Daniel asked, "Does it really say 'his'?"

Jayne passed it to him, and Daniel studied the paper. "How . . . apropos."

"Let's save your fortune for Nicholas' baby book, okay?" Jayne suggested.

Tom slipped the little paper into his wallet. Then we paid the bill and drove our friends back to the hospital to pick up their car. We hugged and shook hands in the parking lot, Mima and Daniel bursting with good spirits on our behalf. Our friends drove off, and we started toward the hospital doors, Tom's arm tightly around Jayne's waist.

Our joy, it seemed, knew no bounds. We couldn't wait to see our son—Nicholas—to whisper our goodnights.

Chapter Three

We walked jauntily down the hall past the Labor and Delivery suite and slipped into the scrub room. As we stepped into the nursery, our attention was riveted by the increased activity in the intensive care area, enclosed behind glass. As we passed by, we were shocked to see Nicholas, surrounded by a doctor and several busy nurses. One of them spotted us, came out, and quickly led us into the parents' waiting room. All she could tell us was, "The doctor will be in to explain as soon as he can. Please try not to be alarmed."

What on earth was going on? What was wrong with Nicholas? He was perfectly healthy when we left for dinner—just two hours before. From the waiting room, we watched the activity continue over our little boy's tiny body. The doctor's expression was grim. A nurse hung an IV bottle, and another nurse connected it to a line already in his wrist. Our little Nicholas was terribly sick, but for over an hour all we could do was sit looking at one another, now and then speculating in hoarse whispers and making hopeful remarks. Mostly we were quiet, lost in our own thoughts. Occasionally a nurse poked her head in to share some encouraging words.

"Can you tell us what's going on?" we'd ask.

"No, I'm sorry. Dr. Marks will be in soon."

The fear kept growing, filling the small room. There was nothing for us to do but sit and wait, our spirits sinking.

At eleven Ann, the nurse who had been caring for Nicholas when we left for dinner, came in and sat with us briefly. She explained—finally—that Nicholas' temperature had dropped suddenly about eight o'clock, so the doctor on call for our pediatrician had come in. He had examined Nicholas and requested that Dr. Allan Marks, a neonatal critical care specialist, be called in. Jayne nodded; she knew of Dr. Marks, but they'd never had an opportunity to work together.

At one o'clock, looking haggard and pale, Dr. Marks came to speak to us. His dark hair needed combing, his mask hung loosely around his neck, and his yellow gown was rumpled. He pushed up his John Lennon–style antique glasses to rub his eyes, then sank into a chair.

"Your son's muscle tone became weak," he began wearily. "His temperature fell quickly. His respirations grew rapid and his heart rate slowed. We put him into a radiant warmer bed to try to get his temperature up, but after one look at him I did a lumbar puncture to extract some spinal fluid to test for blood cell count. We also had a chest X-ray done, and lots of lab work, including blood cultures to determine whether his illness is bacterial or viral. We think he has a touch of pneumonia, but it's a little too early to tell. It may even be meningitis, or he could have an infection in his blood. We inserted a line into his umbilical artery to monitor his blood pressure, and we started him on antibiotics to cover him in case it's bacterial. I asked his birthmother if she's had any recent illness. She said she had a low-grade fever and a cough and was sneezing a couple of days ago; it looks as if *that* was a common upper-respiratory infection. However, there's no way of telling at this point if that has any bearing here.

"I also had her sign the permit for the lumbar puncture, but she told me that she feels you're his parents and she wants you to sign for everything from now on. I'm told, though, that you can sign medical permits only after you have custody of Nicholas. So as long as he's in this hospital, she'll have to sign. I want you to know that I'm doing all that I can for your son and will keep you posted as we get all the results back. I'm going to look at his X-ray now, and I'll be back up to see you."

"Doctor," Tom said, "may we go in to see him now?"

"Of course, and then I think you should both go home and get some sleep. We'll take good care of him and phone you right away should his condition worsen."

We washed our hands again and put on masks, as Nicholas was now in isolation. We approached his bed with great trepidation. The large heat lamp overhead kept it brightly lit. Nicholas lay flat on his back, his arms stretched out to the sides with his forearms bent up at the elbow. Strips of gauze were loosely tied around his wrists and ankles and safety-pinned to the mattress. The bed was tilted so that Nicholas lay quarterway between a horizontal and a vertical position. He was pale, and his little head had fallen to one side. Tom's first thought as he approached was, *Oh, my God, he looks crucified.*

Despite appearances, Nicholas' hands and feet were simply restrained so that he wouldn't move suddenly and pull out the lines and wires. The nurses explained that the heart-shaped gold-foil probe he wore on his chest monitored the temperature of the overhead light that kept Nicholas warm but not too warm. He also had electrocardiogram leads on his chest to monitor his heart rate and respirations, and two tubes, one into his umbilicus, the other into his right wrist. He had tape on his left heel covering the spot where they had drawn blood. He appeared to be asleep.

"His body temperature is two degrees warmer than when this all began," said one of the nurses. For the moment, all seemed stable. We held his little hands, and his fingers folded over ours. We stroked his forehead.

"We love you, Nicholas," Jayne said, fighting back tears. "We're proud of how brave you are, and we want you to get better."

We spoke to him as if he understood us, explaining why the doctors and nurses had to do what they were doing. He stirred gently and opened his eyes, which had lost their sparkle. We stayed with him until after two in the morning, most of the time with his little fingers wrapped around one of ours. Reluctantly we prepared to leave. We said our goodnights with confusion in our hearts and tears in our eyes. The nurses assured us that they'd call us if he took a turn for the worse during the night.

We saw Dr. Marks as we left the nursery. He said, "The chest X-ray had a shadow on it that could be pneumonia. The results from the lumbar puncture are inconclusive. It's just too early to tell why Nicholas is sick. The next few days will be important in determining just what's wrong."

We thanked him for all his efforts and went to degown. We returned to the parents' room and held one another tightly, weeping. How could this be happening to this dear little boy who for nearly a day now had been our son? Why our son? Why Nicholas? Our questions turned to prayers, and we implored the Lord to restore our son's health and give us the courage to accept his plan for our family. We left the hospital feeling numb with exhaustion, fear, frustration, and grief. Clearly we had known the height of happiness and the nadir of despair in the previous twenty-two hours.

We lived only five minutes from the hospital and were soon home. Our thoughts, however, were back with our little boy. We snuggled close, again thanked the Lord for bringing us a son, and asked that his health would return quickly. After a brief, restless sleep, we were up at six-thirty and soon back at the hospital. The nurses said that Nicholas had slept well and was ready for a visit from his mom and dad.

Nicholas seemed to hear us as we spoke our good mornings. He was still restrained but able to turn his head toward us as we spoke. He was pinker, and some of the cheerfulness had returned to his eyes. We stroked his forehead and held his hands. He wasn't able to eat yet but enjoyed the nipple pacifier the nurses had made for him.

We sat with him for the next several hours, discussing every little thing under the sun: how much we wanted him; how we wanted to take him home to meet Kipling; how sunbeams looked through a misty forest canopy; how there was a big world out there to explore. Often we would look at one another, shake our heads in unison, and smile weakly. Sometimes when there wasn't a nurse within earshot, we spoke our thoughts out loud: "Can you believe that this is really happening? It isn't fair! Why is this innocent child having to go through so much?"

On the morning of February 17, the arterial line into Nicholas' umbilicus was removed, though his head had been partially shaved and an IV started in his scalp. To protect the IV, the nurses had taped a styrofoam coffee cup upside-down over the needle. Then the bottom had been cut out of the cup in a zigzag pattern to form a little crown. Our little boy had become a prince!

More important, this meant that we could hold and feed him again; the scalp IV wasn't quite as delicate as the previous one had been. Jayne got to hold him first. He fed well—one ounce—and he was alert and eager to look around.

Jayne's best friend, Katie, came to meet Nicholas that afternoon. It was a special visit, because she and Jayne had been pals since they were fifteen years old in high school. Katie—tall, slender, and refined, with long brown hair—stood comfortably by Nicholas' bed. "He's so handsome," she exclaimed, "and his hands and feet are so cute."

"He certainly is good-looking," Jayne agreed. "There's no doubt about that. And nearly everyone comments on his hands and feet."

"Oh, Jayne, I don't think our lives will ever be the same again. Now we have a little buddy to pal around with us!"

Katie was a registered nurse who, since her marriage nearly two years before, had specialized in volunteer hospice nursing. She was impressed with how "high tech" District Hospital's new Intensive Care Nursery (ICN) was. At one point, as Jayne was cuddling her son and feeding him, Katie burst out laughing and said "I can't believe my best friend is a *mother*. All those years we babysat together I always knew you'd have children someday, and now look at you—it's as if you'd always had this boy. You're so relaxed and natural with him."

Jayne chuckled, looking from Katie's warm smile to her bright-eyed son lustily sucking on his bottle. After a moment she became serious. "Oh, Katie, I do hope I'll be a good mother. Holding a precious baby is the easy part. Nurture and care come naturally. Consistent parenting is the challenge; applying discipline and gently molding a child into a responsible and credible person—that's the hard part! Tom and I will do our best together, and as long as we approach parenthood as we did marriage—as a team—I'm almost sure we'll be okay. Promise me one thing, though, Katie. If you ever see us spoiling Nicholas, *please* tell us, okay?"

"I promise, Jayne," Katie replied. "And now, Nicholas, Auntie Katie is going to hold you for the first time."

❧

On Monday Dr. Marks removed Nicholas' IV. Many visitors came by the nursery to meet our little boy. They'd peer in at him through the glass and make faces as they pointed and giggled. We were touched that so many friends and co-workers seemed interested. Jayne's parents came by and were thrilled to welcome their second grandchild into the family. Tom's brother, Rodger, and his wife, Laura, also visited. We asked Rodger if he'd be Nicholas' godfather, and he readily agreed. Jayne's sister, Carolyn, brought by our son's first pair of shoes—baby-size black-and-white oxfords!—and she agreed to be Nicholas' godmother.

Wednesday morning Dr. Marks discontinued the heart monitor, and Nicholas began to establish a schedule for himself. He enjoyed listening to his little pillow-wrapped music box—our first gift to him—and holding the nose of a little stuffed pig that Jayne's mom had brought him. He'd drift off to sound sleep for a full four hours, then take three ounces of formula eagerly. To our delight, Dr. Marks told us that if all continued to go well, he'd discharge Nicholas on Saturday morning, after he'd completed his seven-day course of antibiotics.

Thursday dawned brightly, and Tom went to the hospital to give Nicholas his morning bottle. Jayne stayed home to set up the nursery in what had been our office and organize all the precious and practical gifts we'd received. Her mom came over midmorning to help. Numerous outfits—from newborn sailor suits to size 2 overalls—were sorted into drawers and closets. Beatrix Potter prints were hung on the walls. The changing table was set up. When Tom returned, he found the room transformed. In its center stood a special family tradition—the white wicker bassinet that Jayne, her mother, and numerous other children and grandchildren had slept in. We were ready to welcome our little prince!

At three-thirty Jayne's only brother, Stann, his wife, Missy, and their five-week-old son, Christopher—Jayne's godchild—arrived. We were all just getting ready to leave for a full-scale visit to the hospital when the phone rang. Jayne answered it in the kitchen. It was the charge nurse.

"Jayne, come to the nursery right away. Nicholas' condition has suddenly deteriorated. Dr. Marks wants him transferred to Stanford Hospital immediately. An emergency transport team is on its way."

Chapter Four

Less than ten minutes later, we raced up the back stairs of District Hospital to the nursery on the fourth floor. Joyce, the charge nurse, filled us in. "Nicholas spiked a temperature about three o'clock and wouldn't take fluids. He'd become lethargic and his color went bad again. We called Dr. Marks. He's with Nicholas now."

We entered the ICN. As we stood at Nicholas' side, looking down at his frail little form, we listened to Dr. Marks. "I repeated the spinal tap, and this time the results were positive for meningitis. The question remains, however: Is this a bacterial or a viral infection? I called Dr. David Stevenson, a neonatologist at Stanford. He agreed that an emergency transfer to Stanford's Intensive Care Nursery is your son's best chance. A critical care transport team is on its way."

Jayne began crying uncontrollably. Tom put his arm tightly around her shoulder. She said, "I want him baptized before he leaves."

One of the nurses rushed out to phone for the hospital chaplain. In a few minutes, she returned. "A priest is on his way," she said.

Jayne thanked her, then phoned her mom to update her and ask her to come in for the baptism. Nicholas' two nurses were busy starting new IVs and medications. As they worked, they offered encouragement.

"Stanford will give him the very best that medical science can offer," said Joyce. "He'll be all right, you'll see."

"Stanford has one of the best intensive care nurseries in the country," said Cathy, another of Jayne's pals. "It'll work out."

Fr. Kaylor, a serious young priest, soon arrived. He spoke gently, his voice and eyes full of a compassion that underscored the importance of the sacrament he was about to perform. "You understand that what we're about to give your son can never be taken away—in life or in death." It was a statement, not a question.

Jayne's mom entered just then, worry and concern written on her face. In a moment, the four of us circled around Nicholas. His eyes were closed and he sucked gently on his pacifier.

Fr. Kaylor asked, "Jayne and Tom, what name have you given this child?" A baby began crying in one of the far rooms.

"Nicholas Lawrence," we said in unison.

"What do you ask of God's church for Nicholas Lawrence?"

"Baptism," came our solemn reply.

There followed a reading of Matthew 28:20. The final line filled our sadness with hope: "And know that I am with you always, until the end of the world."

The priest anointed Nicholas' chest with fragrant oil of catechumens, and after a series of prayers and questions and answers whereby we professed our faith and our intentions, he poured water from a vial onto Nicholas' forehead. Joyce stepped over and caught the water in a small pan.

"Nicholas Lawrence, I baptize you in the name of the Father, and of the Son, and of the Holy Spirit."

Nicholas' eyelids fluttered as the cool water touched his forehead. Then Fr. Kaylor silently anointed the crown of his head with golden chrism.

Our son was now baptized into the new life of Christ and welcomed into the Christian community. His alertness during his first religious experience gave us hope. All that could possibly be done had been done. We thanked Fr. Kaylor profusely as he left.

"I'll keep Nicholas and both of you in my prayers," he said shyly, showing us his infectious smile. "May God bless all of you."

The Stanford team of three neonatal specialists—a doctor, a nurse, and a respiratory therapist—arrived moments later and began their assessment. As Dr. Marks quickly updated them, they moved Nicholas from the radiant warmer bed to a transport cart equipped with oxygen, a heart monitor, and a respirator. He looked so vulnerable surrounded by the cocoon of high-tech gadgetry.

As we followed them in our car to Stanford, we reached one of the lowest points in our lives. The road was dark and quiet; there were few other cars. Neither of us spoke for miles. The lights were on in the ambulance ahead, and we could see figures moving around. Tom drove the car, but his thoughts weren't on the road. Anguish—a hurt that was almost physical—welled up inside him. Why was his son in that ambulance? Why was he on the edge of death? Why were we following him in the dead of night? What was he *doing going to another hospital*? Tom pounded the steering wheel and cried out, "How can this be happening? Our *son* is in that ambulance. Why us? I'm so scared for him. Please, Lord, make him well!" Jayne reached out her hand for his and squeezed hard. She couldn't speak. Salty tears streamed down her cheeks.

We followed the ambulance all the way to Stanford's emergency entrance. The moment the vehicle stopped, several people rushed out of the building to assist. Seeing that Nicholas was in good hands, and knowing that there was nothing we could do for him just then, we parked the car and went around to the lobby to register. We passed a crew of janitors scattering carpet cleaner on the floor and vacuuming. The lobby was filled with the smell of artificial pine and the roar of vacuums. We stepped up to the only clerk on duty.

"Hello, we're the Millers, here to register our son."

"Oh, yes, Baby Boy Holt, isn't it?"

We were surprised by this show of efficiency.

"Yes," Tom said. "However, he should be admitted as Nicholas Lawrence Miller. We're adopting him, and that's his name."

"I see," said the clerk, who quickly typed his name, then filled in the rest of the form, all the time asking us questions. When she finished, she handed us a copy. We'd never seen Nicholas' name on an official form before. Just seeing his name typed gave us a tingling sensation. Despite our pain and fear and confusion, that moment was a split-second taste of the joy and celebration of parenting.

Five minutes later, we were being briefed by the East Nursery clerk, who told us that Nicholas was just being assessed and transferred to a new radiant warmer bed. As we waited in the visitors' lounge outside the swinging doors to the nursery, a patient/family-support volunteer greeted us and began an orientation to Stanford Hospital and its Intensive Care Nursery (ICN). Although our minds were on our little boy, we tried to pay attention as she diligently showed us where we could freshen up and brought us beverages. We were so distracted that we probably seemed unappreciative and brusque. Only much later did we learn that she had been called in from her home especially to help us.

Soon after, Christine, the cheerful blond nurse who had helped to transport Nicholas, peeked through the doors and motioned to us to come through.

"You can go in and see your son now," she said. "I'll be his primary nurse from now on. He appears stable at this time. Several doctors are on their way in to examine him. We'll keep you informed about how they feel he's doing."

Chris also explained the visiting routine to us. We'd be expected to scrub and gown before entering the nursery, where nearly forty cribs and bassinets stood dormitory-style against the two long walls. When approaching Nicholas' bed, we'd have to put on elastic gloves before having any contact with him. Because there was a chance he was infectious, we'd be required to remain within a seven-by-five-foot space marked off by red tape on the floor. This was called "enteric isolation." Before we stepped out over the tape, we would have to remove our gowns and gloves and discard them in receptacles kept within the taped boundary. To cross back over the tape into isolation required rescrubbing, regowning, and regloving. Visiting was allowed all day and evening, except when the doctors were making morning and afternoon rounds. Phone calls into the nursery were encouraged at any time around the clock.

Despite the fact that thirty or more infants were in cribs in the same room as Nicholas, that night our eyes were on only our little boy. He was on his back and restrained much as he had been at

District Hospital. Because he might need to be instantly assessed at any given moment, he was completely naked. A little plastic bag over his penis collected urine for measurement and analysis. The heart-shaped metallic probe on his chest and the heat lamp over his bed worked together to keep him warm.

The air droned with the combined sound of forty monitors beeping constantly, and nearly as many respirators hissing. No fewer than two dozen MDs, RNs, and respiratory therapists were in attendance, most racing around calling out updated information to one other. But it was impossible to tell who was who from their dress. Except for those few who wore yellow gowns with patients in isolation, everybody dressed in uniformly drab and anonymous gray-green scrubs.

We'd been with Nicholas only a few minutes, telling him what was going on and that we wanted him to be brave, that we loved him and cared about him, when the intern, resident, and senior fellow came over to examine him. As they scrubbed at the nearby sink, lathering the pungently sweet pink soap all over their hands and arms, they introduced themselves. They put on fresh gowns as we pulled off ours. Then we stepped out of isolation. As we left the nursery, the neonatologist, Dr. David Stevenson, stopped us and introduced himself. Jayne had attended a seminar he'd given at District Hospital and recognized him immediately. He stood well over six feet, had features handsome enough to grace the cover of *Gentlemen's Quarterly,* and smiled easily over a deep cleft in his chin. He explained that he was one of three primary neonatologists on staff and that he'd be attending Nicholas for the rest of the month. Then he joined the doctors at Nicholas' bedside.

We went out to the lounge to await word. It was the end of the day and the carpet and chairs were filthy with litter and cigarette ashes. A whole family of smokers sat opposite us, waiting, as we were, for word about their loved one. In their nervousness, they sucked and puffed and coughed, filling the area with dizzying clouds of acrid smoke. Feeling like limp rag dolls, we waited. Our minds were devoid of everything except for a numbing mixture of abstract hope and fear, awareness of exhaustion setting in, and the fervent wish that the other people would just *go away*. After a half-hour, Dr. Stevenson came out.

"Nicholas *does* have aseptic meningitis," he said. "We'll be doing many lab tests and taking X-rays to determine if anything else is wrong. He's receiving intravenous antibiotics and other medications, and the infectious disease specialists have been called in. Tomorrow they should have a much clearer idea of Nicholas' prognosis. He'll need to remain in isolation until we know just what 'bug' is causing his problems."

We thanked him. Then, as the doctor turned to walk off, Tom asked, "You wouldn't be related to Robert Louis Stevenson, would you, Doctor?" The question was totally spontaneous—his attempt to grasp something familiar in an otherwise insane tableau.

Instead of revealing the blank expression one would expect, the doctor paused in thought, rubbing his chin. "You know, I believe he *does* have a connection with my family somehow." Then he shrugged and continued on his way.

Before Jayne had a chance to open her mouth, Tom said, "Don't ask. God knows why I said that."

Jayne looked up at her husband with a loving grin. "I think we're both exhausted—that's why."

We went through the scrub routine and returned to Nicholas' bedside, where Chris was busy drawing medications into syringes, adjusting IV flows, checking monitors, and charting.

As she worked, she explained, "There'll be a nurse with Nick around the clock. He won't be left alone even for a minute."

"As busy as you are," Tom said, "I can see Nicholas is going to keep you guys hopping. Oh, by the way, Chris—and please don't misunderstand—his name is Nicholas, not Nick or Nicky."

"I see. Okay, I'll make a note of that on his chart so that the other nurses will know."

"Thank you, Chris. We appreciate that," Jayne said.

From the day we chose our son's name seven years before, we had known that the pet forms of Nicholas simply wouldn't do. On the one hand, Jayne loved her grandfather—after whom our son received his first name—too much to hear his name diminished.

On the other, neither of us could bear the thought of our boy being called "Nick-eeee" as he grew into strapping manhood. Though we knew it would be a hard and perhaps never-ending battle, we were determined that Nicholas would be called *Nicholas* as long as we had anything to do with it.

We gazed down at our baby. His fingers and head moved listlessly. Only seven days old, and it seemed to us he'd already been through a war. Here he lay, requiring care that only one of the most sophisticated, state-of-the-art hospitals in the world could give. Looking at his delicate, pale little body—under a wild confusion of lines, wires, tubes, and needles, connected to syringes, pumps, bottles, and monitors—it was inconceivable that his problems might only be beginning.

We sat there on tall stools, one on either side of his warmer bed. Jayne held his right hand, Tom his left.

"You're going to make it, little guy," Jayne said. "You're loved, and we want you."

"We're fighting to make you well, Nicholas," said Tom, "and you're *going* to make it, because we're *here* for you. Please get better, my son."

Without ever being told, we knew in our hearts the absolute bottom-line importance of staying with him—of whispering to him and talking and singing, of touching and constantly reinforcing to him that we were *there*. Reinforcing that whatever might happen, *we were the constant in his life and we loved him,* that above all else *we wanted him.*

We emphasized *wanting* him because we sensed that somehow he'd picked up his birthmother's feelings—that he was *not wanted* and perhaps *resented*. We felt an urgency to counteract those feelings. If he was going to make it, *he had to know he was wanted!*

Finally, at one-thirty in the morning, after the nurses had changed shifts and we'd met the night nurse, Mary, we stroked our little boy's forehead, squeezed his hands, and said goodnight. We knew that we couldn't help Nicholas if we were sick ourselves from exhaustion, but even so we felt guilty for leaving. Mary seemed to sense this and encouraged us to call in at any time to check. "Thank you, Mary," Jayne said. "But please understand that we need to be kept informed. If there's any change for better or for worse, whether minor or important, please don't hesitate to call us, regardless of the time. Okay?"

Mary nodded thoughtfully. "Don't concern yourselves about that," she said. "If anything happens, I'll be sure you're called immediately." We left the hospital feeling confident Mary understood that we needed to be Nicholas' advocates.

On the way home, we discussed our feelings.

"I don't get it," Tom said. "Why is Nicholas so sick? He was perfect at birth. It doesn't make any sense."

"Well, his birthmother didn't have any prenatal care," Jayne thought aloud. "Lord knows if she took vitamins. But you're right. It doesn't make sense."

"Then maybe if she'd taken better care of herself, Nicholas wouldn't be going through this."

Jayne sighed deeply. "I don't know. We don't even know what's making him ill. There's no point getting angry."

She heard herself say the words, but she didn't believe them for a second. She had plenty of reason to be angry. Our beautiful newborn son was *dying*. Why? Was it because his mom hadn't taken care of him? It seemed the logical explanation. But if she valued life enough not to abort the child, why wouldn't she have taken care of him? The questions whirled in Jayne's mind, but there were no answers. Later perhaps, but not then.

At six the next morning, Jayne hopped out of bed and called the nursery.

"Nicholas slept peacefully through the night," Mary said. "We're all cheering him on."

At seven Dr. Marks, who was still Nicholas' primary physician, called us after having seen our son at Stanford.

"Nicholas' condition is stable. I'm hoping that some new antibiotics I've ordered will do the trick."

These early-morning phone calls from Dr. Marks had become a daily routine for us and helped us to start the day aware of our son's progress. We were grateful for his thoroughness and kindness.

By eight we were back at the hospital. Nicholas was awake and looked better to us. We settled ourselves in for the day, once again sitting opposite one another with Nicholas between. Because we couldn't bring books, magazines, or baby toys into isolation, we had only our imaginations to keep ourselves and our son occupied.

"Life is an adventure, Nicholas," Jayne reminded her little boy, "a wonderful adventure full of many things to see and do. We'll play in the park, and when you get older we'll go on trips."

"But we don't always have to go somewhere," Tom added. "There are books to read and records to listen to, movies to see."

"Nick-Nick-Nick-Nicholas . . . you're a little boy named Nicholas . . . I love a little boy named Nicholas . . . yes, I *do* and daddy does, *too* . . . we—love—*you*!"

"There's a whole big world out there to explore, little guy. We'll help you and be with you, just as we are right now. You're going to make it!"

"And you have so many aunts and uncles and grandparents and friends who are excited to meet you and play with you."

Our entreaties, our pep talks, our positive thoughts, our hand-holding went on and on. Our repertoire of songs grew to include "The Mickey Mouse Club Song," "Frère Jacques," and "Twinkle, Twinkle, Little Star."

At the other end of the nursery, a nurse often played a Lionel Richie tape. One tune in particular—"All Night Long"—struck a chord with Jayne. The line "We're going to have a party!" became her theme for Nicholas' recovery. In days to come, whenever the tape played in the background—which was frequently—she sang the line with a bright sparkle in her eye, keeping rhythm with her finger and pointing in time at her little boy: "Nicholas, we're going to have a party!"

We also tried the visualizing technique of conjuring up in our mind's eye the bugs that were hurting him and then destroying them. We'd read articles that lent support to the strength of this kind of focused positive energy. Feeling that it couldn't hurt, we kept it up for his entire stay at Stanford.

And we did all this inside isolation, with the ever-present full-time nurse bustling around us, drawing medicines into syringes, cleaning IV connections, replacing monitor leads, and all the rest. At noon Katie came to visit, and Tom went out to the lounge. Stanford was strict about enforcing its "two visitors only" rule. Katie and Jayne kept Nicholas company for a couple of hours, holding his hands and winding the specially sterilized music box that had been our first gift to him back at District Hospital. Wrapped in a little pillow embroidered with a giraffe and baby blocks spelling out the words I AM LOVED, it played Brahms' "Lullaby." About this time a running joke began: when Nicholas came through this, he'd probably loathe Brahms' "Lullaby"!

After Katie went home, we left; afternoon rounds had begun, and we needed to honor the privacy rule. Because the ward was completely open, it was considered improper to let visitors at adjoining beds overhear the doctors as they discussed the details of a case.

At three-thirty, Dr. Terry Sweeney, the senior fellow, phoned our home. "I've observed irregularities in Nicholas' breathing," he said. "I don't want to take any chances. I want to insert a breathing tube so that his breathing can be assisted by a respirator."

Despite the fact that working with breathing tubes and respirators was Jayne's career, it shocked her greatly to know that our little boy required such drastic action. Nonetheless, she trusted the doctor's decision. Tears ran down her cheeks and her voice quivered, though she tried to remain in control.

"If you feel it's best, Doctor. We'll be right back in. And thank you so much for taking the time to call."

Dr. Sweeney met us in the hall as we approached the East

Nursery. "Nicholas has been intubated and is on a respirator," he said. "He's been given Pavulon, a medication that prevents him from fighting the respirator and pulling out the breathing tube. In effect, it's paralyzed him, and we'll need to keep him on it as long as he's on the respirator. For someone on Pavulon, of the five senses only the sense of hearing remains intact. You'll see that he's completely motionless."

As pale as we'd seen Nicholas in recent days, this was the worst. His head was turned to the left, and the breathing tube was in his mouth, taped across his upper lip and both cheeks.

"He's terribly still," said Tom. He had to look at the heart and respiratory monitors above the bed to confirm that his son was still alive.

"All I know, darling," Jayne said, "is that it's more important than ever that we talk softly to Nicholas and reinforce our love for him. He probably can still hear us. In fact, that's all he has now."

What *can* you say or feel when you see your son so completely motionless—so completely paralyzed—attached to a respirator and connected up to more IV bottles, monitors, and syringes than you ever imagined possible? The mental fatigue is almost physical. The helplessness grows, and hopelessness gains ground.

We found ourselves looking at each other, searching the eyes for some flicker of belief that all the trust we put in God and the doctors would not be in vain, but seeing only mirror images of our own strained, drawn, infinitely tired expressions.

At five-fifteen, Jayne slipped out to the lobby to meet her brother and his wife, who wanted to meet their nephew. Jayne explained that there was a "two visitors only" rule and that Nicholas had a breathing tube in place and was on a respirator. They all agreed that Missy should stay behind with Christopher. As Jayne showed Stann how to scrub and gown, he watched intensely and followed her example, asking questions. "What about fingernails?" "Scrub for three *full* minutes?" "Am I lathered enough?" He wanted to be sure that he did everything correctly. Then they entered the nursery. As Jayne showed him where to find the elastic gloves on the central counter, Tom stepped out of isolation and exchanged a few words with his brother-in-law. There wasn't an awful lot to say. Stann, a father himself for only six weeks, looked down at Nicholas for a long time. He put his arm around his sister and shook his head. Finally he said, in sadness and confusion, "It just isn't fair. How come a little kid has to go through this?"

At a little before seven, we were waiting in the nonsmoking lounge at the far end of the third-floor corridor to see the infectious disease specialist, Dr. Pamela Diaz.

"Dr. Buckley, 4353 please. Dr. James Buckley to 4353." The halls reverberated with the ubiquitous pages. "Dr. Sheehan to the O.R. please. Dr. Dennis Sheehan to the O.R."

Dr. Diaz hadn't arrived yet, and we took the opportunity to hold one another tightly. "Oh, Tommy, what are we going to do if we lose Nicholas? I love him so. He's such a brave little boy to be going through so much. But we have to ask ourselves, *What are we going to do if we lose him?*"

"I don't know; but I *do* know that we can't let it affect us—I mean you and me as a couple. We have to somehow keep a *united front.* I know that's important. We'll just have to survive somehow." Tom looked from Jayne to the tiled ceiling. *"It's not right!* How can God give us Nicholas, and then let him get sick like this? It's not fair!"

Her head resting on Tom's chest, Jayne was aware of the faint smell of aftershave and somehow felt a little more secure because of it. She said quietly, "I guess we just have to be as brave as he is."

Just then Dr. Diaz came down the hall to explain what Nicholas' tests had shown so far. "Since a bacteria hasn't been identified, we're most suspicious of a viral infection. Viruses are very hard to culture, because they don't live long outside their hosts. I spoke to Nicholas' birthmother earlier, and she denies any history of herpes, but in a baby this young, who's been ill since birth, that's always a primary consideration. We're going to do a CAT scan of his brain now. Usually herpes encephalitis shows up as a lesion in the left temporal lobe. If the CAT scan isn't conclusive, we'll probably want to do a brain biopsy. Right now Nicholas is being placed in a small transport cart to go to the X-Ray department." She then went off to be present during the CAT scan.

Shaken, Jayne went to a nearby pay phone. Her mother and friends and all the prayer chains that were praying for Nicholas across the country had to be updated. But before she began to describe our son's condition and the procedures that the doctors felt were necessary, she asked her mom to do a favor.

"Mom, please call Katie and Mima and pass this info on to them. I'm just too exhausted—utterly fatigued—and I don't think I can tell all of this story more than once.

"Nicholas is down having a brain scan right now, and we're very frightened for him. They tell us that after the brain scan, they'll probably want to do a brain biopsy. Can you imagine? They want to stick a needle into our one-week-old son's brain. Mom, I'm so scared and so angry. Why is God making Nicholas go through this?"

"I'm sure you *are* angry, honey," her mother responded. "None of this is fair—not to Nicholas or to you or Tom."

"We don't want to *lose* this baby, Mom. Listen to this. His name is Nicholas Lawrence. Do you know what those names mean? Nicholas means 'victory of the people' and Lawrence means 'crowned with laurel.' Imagine that name! Such strength for a tiny little boy: 'Victory of the people, crowned with laurel'!"

Jayne began to cry again, and her mother quietly asked, "Jayne, what is the *ultimate* victory? Isn't it the gift of eternal life? Nicholas was baptized just yesterday. You've done the best thing possible for him." That reminder of resurrection possessed a special power. That night, and in all the days that followed, it provided a peaceful perspective in the midst of chaos.

Forty-five minutes later, we were still waiting for Nicholas to be returned from the CAT scan. We sat side by side in the lounge with our eyes closed and our heads resting against each other. At the far end of the hall, a janitor guided a whirring polishing machine along the linoleum floor. Jayne opened her eyes briefly, and she became aware of a tall, slim, perfectly poised woman walking down the long hall toward them. It was nearly nine-thirty, and the hospital was growing quiet. She closed her eyes again, thinking, *That woman is unusually nicely dressed and coifed for this late hour.* Her thoughts were interrupted by the words, "Hi, you two!" Her eyes opened and there was her dear friend Katie; Jayne hadn't even recognized her as Katie walked down the hall.

"Katie!" we both shrieked. "What are you doing here?"

"Well, I talked to Jayne's mom, and she said that Nicholas wasn't doing well, so I wanted to come right up and see if I could help you guys out. All I can say is it's awfully lucky the Highway Patrol wasn't out in force tonight!" She smiled impishly. "Now please tell me all about what's happening with—"

Tom broke in: "Katie, you *are* an angel—an honest-to-goodness angel! Coming all that way—it's as if you magically appeared!"

Katie brushed aside these compliments with aplomb. "Oh, before I forget, Mima called just as I was leaving. She'd heard from your mom also, and wanted to know what I knew. She sends her love and says their home is open day and night. There'll always be enough dinner so you won't even have to think about that. Just show up at their front door." Mima and Daniel's love and generosity were like an oasis in the desert! We blessed them heartily (and in days to come often took them up on their offer).

Moments later, after a ninety-minute procedure, Dr. Diaz returned to the lounge, and we introduced Katie.

"Nicholas is being returned to the East Nursery," she told us as she sat down. "The CAT scan showed encephalitis—a general swelling of the brain—but was inconclusive for herpes." She was obviously fatigued, repeatedly running her fingers through her shoulder-length blond hair.

Jayne's fear swelled. She asked, "Since he's already on acyclovir to treat any possible herpes infection, how will doing a biopsy alter the treatment he's receiving?"

Dr. Diaz answered calmly, "The treatment probably *wouldn't* change. But it would be useful to know conclusively whether its herpes or not."

"What are the risks of a brain biopsy?"

"Well, there are several." Just then, the doctor was interrupted by a nurse who drew her aside briefly to discuss some urgent hospital business.

Jayne took this opportunity to turn to Tom and say, "We just can't accept everything the doctors say without questioning. Nicholas needs us to be his advocates. If we aren't, who will be? Even though they have the best intentions, doctors sometimes forget they're dealing with real people." She paused for emphasis. "I simply can't sign a permit for a biopsy. If several days from now they still don't know what's wrong, perhaps I'll reconsider. Right now I think it's an unnecessary intervention just because he *might* have herpes. I think we have to believe his mother when she says she's never had herpes. She's the only one who could've given it to him."

Tom felt a great sense of relief. Jayne was articulating the fears that had consumed his own thoughts since the subject of biopsy had come up. "You're right, darling," he said. "We just can't stand by and allow the doctors to do everything that comes to their minds. Someone has to speak up for Nicholas, and there's no one to do it but us." In his heart, Tom thanked God that Jayne had the medical background and the moxie to follow through. And all the while, Katie stood back, quietly listening.

When Dr. Diaz returned her attention to us, she looked at our concerned faces and nodded her head. "I know this is a difficult decision. It's nearly midnight. Why don't you go in and see Nicholas and consider it?"

The four of us walked down the long hall toward the East Nursery. Tom reached out for Jayne's hand and squeezed it tightly. "I hope we're doing the right thing for Nicholas," he said. We passed through the East Nursery's waiting area and Katie found a seat. We pushed open the double doors of the nursery to peek in at Nicholas before we went into the scrub room.

A dozen busy people clustered around him. Clearly something was very wrong. Dr. Diaz registered as much surprise as we did. She said, "I'll go in and check on what's happening and let you know."

We retreated quietly into the waiting area and slowly sank into the seats next to Katie.

"What could be wrong now?" Jayne groaned helplessly.

Tom said, "You know, this is getting to be like the trap doors in *Alice in Wonderland.* Each crisis is a door we fall through, and before we even have a chance to catch our breath, the floor drops out from beneath us again—and again—and again. Every time we think we've hit rock bottom, the trap door drops open and down we go again. This reeling feeling, as if the wind were being knocked out of us again and again, has got to stop. When will it end? When will our little boy start getting better? I just want him *well!"*

Dr. Diaz came back out and sat on the edge of the upholstered seat in front of us. "He's had a massive double pulmonary hemorrhage." Tom looked at the doctor questioningly, and she saw his confusion. "That means both his lungs have spontaneously filled—exploded, if you will—with blood. It's a good thing he was intubated earlier, or there would have been nothing, nothing at all, we could've done. As it is, it appears touch and go." Her eyes looked sad, and she said softly, "I'm so sorry this is happening to you."

We looked at one another as she left. We could hear the door crashing shut above our heads, and there was a sickening feeling deep in our stomachs.

A flurry of activity followed, and the three of us remained in the waiting area watching staff come and go. We were given only brief updates on Nicholas' progress: "It's still touch and go." "Too soon to tell if he'll make it." "Thank God he'd been tubed earlier." "Hang in there!" "We'll let you know what the next chest X-ray shows." "They think he's stabilizing!" We discussed each and every statement, trying to glean hope from every one.

At some point, a woman with a toddler in tow met a friend in the lounge. As the women talked, the little girl, crawling all over the dirty carpet, picked up a ground-out cigarette butt and put it in her mouth. The woman looked down but didn't seem to notice.

Tom leaned over and whispered to Jayne, "I can't believe I'm seeing what I'm seeing."

Jayne's mouth was agape. Rage at that woman filled us both. How stupid could she be? Didn't she know how fragile her child was? How a virus or bacteria could kill her?

Nicholas was fighting for his life just yards away, and this woman was letting her child eat cigarette butts off the floor! We wanted to scream.

Soon after this, Dr. Marks—still wearing one of District Hospital's yellow gowns—came racing down the hall on his way to the nursery. He spotted us. "I'm sorry," he said. "I'm so sorry." He threw his arms around both of us. We were all too tired, too drained, to speak further.

Then he dashed through the double swinging doors.

Chapter Five

Four in the morning. Nicholas showed no improvement. We went to freshen ourselves, but the faces we saw in the restroom mirrors were barely recognizable as our own: pasty-looking and haggard, our reflections seemed distorted. Were our eyes playing tricks? Even the hospital walls and corridors blurred together.

Periodically we looked through the little windows of the double doors into the nursery but could see only varying numbers of doctors and nurses in green scrubs and yellow gowns bent over the tiny, tube-filled body of our precious Nicholas. Jayne held herself tightly, partly to ward off the chill draft and partly from fear. Tom kept his fists clenched in his pockets. All the while, Katie stuck by us, her mere presence giving us strength and hope we probably wouldn't have had otherwise.

One time Tom asked, "Jayne, do you have a mint or something?"

"No. I'm sorry, I don't."

"But I do," Katie said, grabbing her purse, which looked like a designer doctor's bag. She rummaged in it and produced a package of mint Life Savers. For years, there'd been a running joke between Jayne and Katie that nearly anything anyone would ever need—cookies, candy, Kleenex tissues—Katie could produce Mary Poppins–style from her seemingly bottomless purse.

Katie was clearly and simply our support and morale booster that horrible night.

But we realized finally that there was nothing more we could do. Saying goodnight to Katie and taking a last glance at the activity around Nicholas' bed, we went home.

Saturday loomed overcast and gray. Despite the pall, Nicholas survived the entire day without any major crises. The doctors told us that we should be somewhat optimistic; his heart and kidneys were still working well, and they felt that if they could "buy Nicholas enough time" for the infection to run its course, perhaps he would survive. We clung to this ray of hope.

On Sunday Nicholas showed everybody just what a fighter he was. The doctors thought he was doing well enough that they tried to discontinue his Pavulon—the paralyzing drug—in favor of morphine, which would keep him sedated but capable of movement. As the Pavulon wore off, he kicked and squirmed and tried to get rid of the breathing tube by banging his head from side to side. They immediately readministered Pavulon for his own protection.

Dr. Stevenson gave us the encouraging news. "The fact that he bucked the respirator as hard as he did is a good sign. He has plenty of inner reserve that could help in the long stretch. In a day or so, we'll try again, but next time we'll sedate him first."

Early Monday Tom returned to work from his "vacation"—his plans to relax and finish writing his mystery novel unrealized will-o'-the-wisps. While he was twenty miles away describing the previous week to his stunned supervisors, Jayne stood quietly in the ICN gazing at her son, lost in maternal reverie and memories of days past. A familiar voice returned her to the present. "How are you doing, Jayne?"

She looked up and saw Dr. Rubenstein, Nicholas' pediatrician. "Oh, Laurie, so much has happened. It's wonderful to see you."

"I came over the instant I found out. I'm awfully sorry."

Despite the fact that it wasn't good isolation technique, they hugged, and Jayne struggled to keep from crying. Laurie explained that now that she was back from Mexico she would resume her role as Nicholas' primary physician. Then she set about examining him.

Learning that a detailed examination of his heart hadn't yet been performed, she ordered an immediate electrocardiogram and an echocardiogram, which is an ultrasound examination of the heart. Both showed severely abnormal function. The preliminary diagnosis: myocarditis.

The infection had now reached his heart—having already attacked his blood, brain, spine, and lungs. Lasting damage to his heart muscle was nearly certain. The dark skies and rainy weather fit our sinking, dark moods. Tuesday we stayed by his side all day, whispering our encouragement. New medications were prescribed to control his blood pressure and the irregular heartbeats that had appeared. When technicians did another echocardiogram at his bedside, we got to see his heart beating on a video screen. Even we saw that Nicholas' left ventricle was not opening and closing in a regular rhythm. We returned home late Tuesday night to a few hours of fitful sleep.

At a quarter to five, the phone jarred us awake. Tom answered.

"Mr. Miller," Dr. Stevenson said, "I'm sorry to disturb you at this hour. I wanted you to know that at four o'clock Nicholas had a fifteen-minute episode of ventricular fibrillation."

"I'm sorry, but I don't know what that means," Tom said. He thought, *What on earth is* fibrillation?

"We had to use the defibrillator."

First *fibrillation* and now *defibrillator.* What on earth was this doctor telling him?

"I'm sorry, Doctor. I guess I'm a little groggy. I *really* don't understand. Please tell me what happened to Nicholas."

Dr. Stevenson, controlling his impatience, explained: "That means his heart stopped beating and began to quiver. You can think of it as a kind of heart attack. We had to use the defibrillator—you've seen them, the electric paddles—followed by almost fifteen minutes of CPR."

As Tom began to understand, his own heart speeded up. *Our poor little boy! Please, God, help Nicholas—Help him survive!*

The doctor went on: "Nicholas' potassium level has increased dramatically. We feel that this caused the crisis, as too much potassium can cause the heart to misfire. That means the infection has now reached Nicholas' kidneys. We need your permission to start Nicholas on peritoneal dialysis to lower his potassium level. A tube will be placed in an incision in his abdomen, and through that tube a sterile fluid can flush the affected area."

Tom relayed this awful information to Jayne, concentrating on repeating the unfamiliar medical terms correctly. White with fear and rubbing her forehead intensely, Jayne took the phone. Her brain raced with memories of patients with multiple organ failure who were kept alive through intense medical effort yet without significant restoration of their health—the legacy of all the doctors' efforts being only a tragically poor quality of life during their last days. Eight years of critical care respiratory therapy had taught her that there were limits.

"Dr. Stevenson," she said, "I want to remind you that we're really very concerned about unnecessary medical heroics. We can't have Nicholas' suffering prolonged. Last-ditch efforts are fine—if they stand a real chance. Too often—"

"Mrs. Miller, I assure you that we want only to buy Nicholas some time. If we can keep him alive while this infection runs its course, he has a chance. If he's going to die, this intervention won't prolong his life."

On our way to the hospital, Jayne underscored to Tom how serious Nicholas' fibrillation was. Given everything he had been through, our son was hanging on by the thinnest of threads.

We arrived as the sun was rising, but the tears in our eyes and the waning hope in our hearts made us oblivious to the new light. Before we entered the nursery, we asked the clerk/receptionist to call the hospital chaplain. At Nicholas' bed were two nurses; we were told that as long as he was in isolation and on dialysis he would need two full-time nurses. Jayne stroked our son's forehead and face, tears streaming silently down her face. Tom cried uncontrollably. "Please, God," he whispered, "don't let my son die."

Somehow Jayne rallied long enough to call our attorney, Diane Michelson, at home. "Diane," she said, "if Nicholas' birthmom has any desire at all to see her child, now is the time. He probably won't live out the day."

"I'll call her right away and get back to you at the hospital," Diane said, her normally strong and self-confident voice cracking.

Ten minutes later, Diane called back. "She wanted to know how you guys were holding up. But she said she feels you're his parents now; she won't come to see him. And if he dies, she wants you to make whatever funeral arrangements you choose."

Jayne relayed this information to Tom. Frankly, we were both perplexed by the young woman's ability to distance herself so totally.

The chaplain arrived at six-thirty and was soon anointing Nicholas and praying over his small, colorless body. Chris, his primary nurse, joined us. We held hands and bowed our heads in prayer. Then we also anointed our son, praying fervently that he would be healed.

"Dear Lord," Tom said haltingly, "please protect our son and save him from this terrible affliction."

Then Jayne spoke passionately from the depths of her very being. "God, you once asked Abraham to sacrifice his son for your sake, and Abraham obeyed your will. If you're asking us to do the same, please give us the strength to accept and understand. We're angry, Lord—angry and sad and frightened. We understand that you will probably take our son this day, if that is your will. But if it's at all possible, please let us keep him, as you allowed Abraham to keep Isaac."

The four of us chorused a subdued "Amen," feeling that despite everything, we were probably going to lose Nicholas that day.

Though with part of our minds we pleaded with God to restore our little boy to us, another part sought answers to all that was happening. These events simply made no sense. When Nicholas entered our lives, we felt in our hearts that we three had come together for a reason. Now we considered the possibility of his being taken from us. Why? What was it all about? Why was this precious baby—this gift from God—given into our care only to be yanked away so quickly? Was it to teach us something from the experience? If so, what was the lesson? It was hard, so very hard. Where was the sense in it?

The nursery staff looked on sympathetically. Mary, the night

nurse who was going off duty, told us she would come back in to
be with us when he died.

ক্ষ

Against all the odds, he hung on. By nine that evening, when
we went down the hall for a break, we were once again hopeful.
He was deathly ill, we knew, but somehow he had survived another precarious day. In our minds, mere survival had come to
equal hope.

When we returned to the nursery, we glanced over at Nicholas'
bed before going into the scrub room. A very tall man with unruly
dark brown hair stood looking down at Nicholas.

"What now?" Jayne groaned. "Tom, have you ever seen that
doctor before?"

Just then the "doctor" turned around and we saw a Roman
collar peeking above the yellow hospital gown. This lean, thin-
faced, somewhat disheveled-looking priest saw us, conferred with
a nurse who looked our way and nodded, then walked briskly in
our direction. Neither of us knew him, but when Jayne heard him
utter his farewell to the nurses, she recognized the deep, resonant
voice she had spoken to so often in the weeks before Nicholas
entered our lives. Fr. James Dempsey threw his long arms around
us both and said, "I just baptized your son. Now he's an honorary
Dempsey kid. Let's go out and get acquainted. I want to hear all
about what you and Nicholas have been through."

Through a cloud of exhaustion—partly galvanized, partly mes-
merized by the priest's powerful presence—Jayne thought back,
remembering the encouragement this man had offered over the
phone during the final six weeks of our adoption search. Though
he hadn't been involved in Nicholas' placement, Fr. Dempsey had
been instrumental in approximately thirty adoptions in twenty-
four years. As a faculty member of the Theater and Communication Arts Department at the University of San Francisco, a Jesuit
school, he came into contact with both sides of the adoption

scenario—students, pregnant and confused, who didn't know what to do, and couples unable to have their own children. He described himself as running an adoption agency out of his back pocket. His only records were pictures of "his kids," which he would gladly pull out and display accordion-style.

Laughter echoed through the quiet hospital halls as Fr. Dempsey punctuated his story of how he often shocked people by showing off "his" children. Now Nicholas' picture would be added to the pack.

"Thank you so much for coming, Father." Tom's voice rose in his excitement. "I can't tell you how unexpected this is. And you baptized Nicholas again! He can use all the help he can get right now."

Jayne reached out and took Tom's hand, affirming the love she felt watching her husband, the proud protective papa.

We gestured to the nurses that we would be nearby and followed Fr. Dempsey out to the smoking lounge, where he threw himself into a chair, stretched out his long legs, and lit an extra-long cigarette. It was difficult to answer his nonstop questions, for as quickly as he'd ask one, leaving us with half-opened mouths and scattered answers, he'd speed on to another thought. "Just how did you find Nicholas?" "Tom, what did you say you do for a living?" "Now what precisely happened at District Hospital?" "And he's been *here* how long?" "How old is he?" "Twelve days— he looks so much older, somehow!" "Tell me how you two met."

Fr. Dempsey soon shared with us that he had cancer—even as he sucked hard on another cigarette—and was walking around today in sheer defiance of a grim prognosis given six years before. He encouraged us to have hope that Nicholas would recover, and commended us as a couple for our intense commitment not only to our young son, but to one another.

He shook his head as he remembered aloud: "I can't tell you the number of couples and whole families that have fallen apart. When confronted with the kinds of things you've dealt with here, most people just lose it. You two folks are something else. I'm proud to know you."

We smiled at his comments. We didn't think we were doing anything special. Our little boy was sick, and we were doing our best to help him. What was special about that? In the weeks to come, however, we would come to a deep understanding of our new friend's point of view.

An hour passed; then one of the senior residents came out of the nursery with a thumbs-up sign to tell us that the dialysis was working. Her wide grin matched our own. With Fr. Dempsey leading, we offered a prayer of thanksgiving.

"Thank you, Heavenly Father, for this ray of hope. Please let it be a bridge to Nicholas' recovery."

As we bid him goodnight, he assured us that he would be in contact with us.

Then Tom asked, "By the way, Father, what brought you here tonight?" We knew that he lived in a residence for priests in the hills of Los Gatos, quite a distance from Stanford. "Oh, I have my ear to the ground all the time, you know, and when I heard there was trouble brewing, I didn't think twice. I just hopped in the old car and, well . . ." He shrugged. "Hell, I'm always driving somewhere! I can't stand sitting around." He winked and strode down the hall as we headed back to the nursery.

The two nurses who were caring for Nicholas that evening chuckled as they told us how fervently Fr. Dempsey had insisted on seeing Nicholas. They allowed him into isolation only because he was a priest and claimed to be a friend of the family. When he asked for water, they explained that Nicholas had already been baptized. His only response was, "That may be, ladies, but I must do it again to make sure it was done right." They brought him some water; he blessed it and baptized Nicholas for a second time.

We stayed with Nicholas until after midnight, then sang our ritual goodnight songs to him—including, of course, the finale: "M-I-C! See you real soon! K-E-Y! Why? Because we *love* you! M-O-U-S-E!"

We didn't know it yet, but this night marked the turning point. Though there would be a number of serious setbacks over the next several weeks, Nicholas got no worse. The trap doors stopped opening out from under us. Each day the world regained a little of its color and sanity.

Whether it was a coincidence or whether Fr. Dempsey carried around a little of God's magic in his hip pocket along with his kids' pictures, we don't know. Regardless, Nicholas' turnabout was wondrously real—and, unknown to us then, there would come a day when we would show our thanks to this wonderful man in a most special way.

～ى

With each succeeding cardiac evaluation, it became clearer that the bug that had nearly killed Nicholas so many different times had left him with a severely damaged heart. During the next seven weeks, the doctors at Stanford treated his heart with a number of medications, mostly for short-term problems. But the life-threatening irregularity of his heartbeats needed constant attention. The first order of business was to find just the right medication to regulate his arrhythmia. After trial and error, the possibilities were finally narrowed down. The potent IV solution lidocaine—*which had never before been used as treatment for a baby*—did the trick. For the remainder of his stay at Stanford, Nicholas received a low dose of lidocaine through a small pump twenty-four hours a day. Any attempt to wean him off it or lessen the dosage sent his heart into tumultuous fits.

At some point, it dawned on us that the rampant infection was one thing, but the damage to his heart was something else entirely. As monstrous as it had been, the infection had come and was now probably going; but the damaged heart it left behind was likely to stay damaged—that is, if Nicholas lived. Somehow we persevered; we were determined to keep our thoughts upbeat.

Laurie Rubenstein came to see Nicholas every day. She was not only our son's pediatrician, but our friend and cheerleader throughout Nicholas' ordeal. She was always honest with us, and we trusted her. We had no doubt, whenever her bright smile dimmed and her eyes filled with tears, that she was on the same rollercoaster with us, that our son's setbacks took their toll on her, too.

One afternoon when Nicholas was about three weeks old, Laurie came looking for us in the hospital cafeteria. She found Jayne sipping tea with Mima.

"Hi, guys. Where's Tom?"

"Hi, Laurie. He's at work."

"So what do you think of your son today?"

"I'm still hopeful, Laurie," Jayne said, "in spite of everything. I'm still carrying that little sailor suit in the car in the hope that he'll soon get to wear his first real outfit." But Laurie knew, for Jayne had insisted on this, that the little suit had a second, sadder function. If Nicholas died, he was to be dressed in it before he was taken to the morgue.

They chatted about other things; then Laurie grew serious. "What about Loma Linda University Medical Center? If things get too bad with Nicholas' heart, what would you think about a baboon heart?"

Jayne remembered the highly publicized Baby Fae case that had made worldwide headlines five months before. She said, "Ideologically, I have no problem with it, but I doubt they'd want to touch a case involving an adopted baby whose birthmother would have to be consulted." Jayne paused, remembering television interviews with Baby Fae's surgeon. Despite the harsh glare of spotlights and the barrage of barbed questions, the doctor had come across as a kind and compassionate man. "If Nicholas gets any worse, though, maybe we should at least try to contact them."

Within days Nicholas improved, and the matter was not discussed further.

◄§

We had hope again. In fact, there was real progress!

About this time, the doctors discontinued the paralyzing Pavulon (though keeping Nicholas sedated for his own protection). With each hour, he regained the ability to move, and five days afterward, he passed his first developmental milestone: he knew his name!

Jayne pointed this out one morning to the examining intern. Grinning shyly, the intern said, "Mrs. Miller, I'm afraid it's just a coincidence. Nicholas is much too young to have learned his name."

Not to be put off, however, Jayne countered cheerfully, "Doctor, please humor me. In a few minutes, call Nicholas by another name, then come back later and call him by his own and see if there's any difference."

The intern came back in about fifteen minutes, looked down at Nicholas as he dozed, and said, "Horatio, Horatio"; she received no response. Again she left the bedside and returned half an hour later for the ultimate test. He was still asleep as she whispered, "Nicholas—oh, Nicholas."

His eyes fluttered open and he turned to her voice. Her eyes grew wide with astonishment, and she broke out into a full smile. "Mrs. Miller," she said, "your son *does* know his name!"

Later that afternoon, Jayne sat by the little bed holding her son's hand, repeating softly, "Strong and steady, Nicholas. Let your heart beat strong and steady. Strong and steady."

As she did so, she reflected on how strangely grateful she was for those seventeen short days we'd known together. She realized that, in all likelihood, those two-and-a-half weeks would've been *taken for granted in normal circumstances*—if Nicholas had left the hospital as expected and had spent nearly three healthy weeks with us at home. Surely we would have loved him and gazed upon him frequently as he slept in his bassinet. We would have fed him, played with him, and cooed over his expressions. But *that* parenting experience was not to be ours.

Instead, our baby was critically ill; our first weeks were not in our sweet nursery at home, but in intensive care. We'd been shown how fragile this child's life was, how precious each and every moment was. Instead of the usual happy, almost passive acceptance of a new member into the family, we'd begun an intensive and deliberate program of *encouragement*—of urging him on!

And clearly these two-and-a-half weeks had yielded results. Nicholas not only lived; he had learned his name! Jayne was struck by the intensity of this new perspective of accomplishment and survival. But she longed, too, for the peace of our quiet home and the joy of watching a healthy baby "just sleep all day" as most newborn infants do.

To commit to parenting Nicholas *fully* despite *everything* lent some specialness to each and every moment of life. There was no doubt in our minds that the experiences we three knew together intensified our bonding—that each of Nicholas' small triumphs and steps toward recovery was accompanied and underscored by our immense pride! Against all the odds, despite all predictions, our little guy was making it!

Parenting creatively became our *raison d'être*—the focal point of our lives. Somehow we always found quality moments to enjoy with our son, despite there being absolutely no privacy. At those times, we told him all about the rainbow of tulips, coral bells, impatiens, and roses blooming in our garden. We kept reminding him—and ourselves—that "life is an adventure, little guy. It's full of fun and exciting things to do!" And we told him about tall mountains and cool lakes and great canyons and Disneyland and Yellowstone National Park and lots of other neat places we'd explore together someday. One night Tom talked with Nicholas for an hour about the stars and planets; it was a mini–astronomy lesson!

"Mars is the fourth planet from the sun, my son. It's called the Red Planet, because it's covered with rust. . . . The middle star of Orion's belt is really an interstellar nursery, where new stars are being born. . . ."

Spending so much time sitting in a forty-crib intensive care unit, we couldn't help but notice the ebb and flow of daily events and routine. Conversations with the omnipresent nurses and respiratory therapists not only gave us a change of pace from our constant encouraging monologue to Nicholas, but also gave us perspective. For example, we noticed early on that we were among the few parents who daily—or even regularly—visited their sick child. At first we thought that we must be missing other parents' visits because we were so wrapped up with our own child. We soon learned, however, that not only was our observation correct, but that *we* were viewed by some of the ICN staff as anomalies. Some pitied us—not for our sick child, but for our misplaced devotion and dedication. In fact, during Nicholas' first two weeks at Stanford, when it was clear to everybody *except us* that we would lose Nicholas, many of the nurses viewed us as "those poor Millers, who were incapable of seeing the writing on the wall."

During those initial weeks, we were counseled by some hospital staff, friends, colleagues, and acquaintances to simply walk away from Nicholas: *since he wasn't really ours, and since we really had no legal obligation to him, there was no reason we couldn't walk out the door and forget the whole episode. Why put ourselves through so much unnecessary trauma? And what for? It was obvious that Nicholas' end was inevitable. Go ahead. Leave. No one would blame you. Besides,* they would always stress, *He's not even yours. Don't be fools.* Such concepts were for us not only unconscionable but also unfathomable.

We weren't angry; we were confused that otherwise fine, well-meaning people could make such outlandish suggestions. *Are they crazy?* we'd think. *Do we live on the same planet?* If we couldn't harbor such thoughts for one second, how could they? One friend even suggested that Nicholas' survival would dilute the gene pool and questioned the morality of our helping him survive. We could only wonder at such remarks.

We also learned—during those early weeks we spent whispering of life's joys to Nicholas—that the majority of parents who experienced the kinds of stresses we were experiencing ended up estranged, separated, or divorced—*if they didn't immediately reject the child because it wasn't perfect.* And more often than not, this was largely due to the husband's inability to deal with the unexpected.

Tom shook his head in disbelief when he heard statements and facts like these. It seemed pretty straightforward to him: Nicholas was terribly sick and needed his parents if he was going to survive. Period.

No other avenue was possible for either of us, for whatever reason—faith, commitment, love, upbringing, some combination . . . who's to say? All we can say for sure is that we know in our hearts that Nicholas' survival then, at the outset of his life, wasn't due entirely to Stanford's heroic doctors and nurses. Our presence, our love for him, our support for him, our *wanting* him to be part of our family were every bit as important!

If we hadn't been there for him, his birthmother still would have given him up, he still would have gotten sick, and he still would have gone to the hospital. He would have become a ward of the state, taken care of by hospital staff who were paid to do so and checked on once a week—at best—over the phone by a county social worker. Yes, the nurses would probably have given him a nickname, but he would still officially have been Baby Boy Holt to all those whose job it was to be interested.

Nicholas simply would never have made it.

Throughout the weeks he spent on a respirator, we couldn't hold him, but we stroked his face and gave him his daily sponge bath. We massaged his feet with lotion, trimmed his nails, washed his hair, and otherwise tended to our little boy as normally as we could.

One motherly touch came as Jayne's response to the aftermath of a number of scalp IVs. Many times, when a nurse wasn't able to start a line in Nicholas' hand or foot successfully, a two-inch-square patch of hair would be shaved from his head and the needle tried in a scalp vein, with varying degrees of success. After a few weeks, Nicholas was mostly bald, with wild little patches of hair poking up here and there where the nurses hadn't bothered to shave. Jayne said he looked as though he'd been scalped with a tomahawk. Tom said that, with a little pink or green hair coloring, he'd make a great punk rocker. One day Jayne had had enough; she asked that his head be completely shaved so that, as he recovered, his hair would grow back evenly.

᪥

At one point, between the crises of Nicholas' pulmonary hemorrhage and his cardiac fibrillation, Jayne had been approached by the hospital's Social Services Department with regard to financial assistance. Being uncertain at the time how much of Nicholas' care would be covered by our personal health insurance, Jayne accepted the suggestion that we contact California Children's Services (CCS), a state department that helps with children's health care payments in certain specific instances. Jayne contacted CCS and was told to bring in our employment, salary, insurance, and tax records for the previous three years, along with an involved, multipage application that they would send us to complete in advance. It seemed like a good deal of work, but since Nicholas' medical bills were mounting rapidly, Jayne asked for the application and made an appointment for the following week.

We'd been through so much that months rather than days seemed to pass between the phone call and the appointment, but finally the day arrived. Jayne showed up at the office bright and early, bearing manila envelopes crammed with the proof of her frustrating and time-consuming labor. When she finally met with the interviewer, the first question the woman asked, without so much as looking at the application, was, "Now let's see, what's your combined gross income?" Jayne told her, and the woman responded sympathetically: "I'm so sorry. Because your income is $2,000 more than the qualifying limit, your application can't be considered." Jayne couldn't believe her ears. Why couldn't they have simply told her what the limits were when she called to make the appointment? She had spent hours filling out the form and researching our personal records—and those things weren't even glanced at by the CCS representative! Besides that, she could have been at the hospital with Nicholas instead of wasting her time!

About this time, we became friends with another couple who daily visited their son in the ICN. Their little boy's name was Kyle Patrick Flynn, and he always wore a tiny baseball cap that his mother had made for him. He was born several weeks prematurely and had an internal abnormality that would require multiple surgeries. We saw them often across the nursery and introduced ourselves to them the morning Kyle had his first operation. They had come in early to see their son before he went to the operating room, and while he had the procedure, the four of us sat in the lounge and talked. Kevin and Mary were both graduate students and, like us, first-time parents. Our friendship grew over the next several weeks—and beyond—as we cheered our little guys toward recovery. Though Kyle was two weeks older, Nicholas was always bigger, so Kyle would eventually get to enjoy Nicholas' hand-me-down clothes.

The dialysis continued to work well, keeping Nicholas' potassium level in the normal range. As Nicholas improved, the procedure was required less and less frequently; he went from twice an hour to once an hour to once every two hours—and so on, for a total of sixteen days.

But on March 10, peritonitis set in. Though we'd been warned at the outset of his dialysis that there was a possibility—even a probability—that a bacterial infection would be introduced through the incision in his abdomen, Nicholas' steady improvement had blinded us to this risk. Peritonitis caused his temperature to rise, his skin to turn gray again, and, worst of all, his belly to swell horribly. In just a matter of hours, Nicholas looked as sick as he had at his worst, if not more so. He grimaced behind his breathing tube and was obviously in pain.

The fear returned. And with it, a raging anger. Despite all the awful things Nicholas had been through, we'd seen him really in pain only when his heels were jabbed daily to obtain blood for testing. As teeth-clenchingly bad as that was, it was quick—over in a minute. This was different; Nicholas was suffering. Jayne couldn't bear it any longer.

Tom watched his wife clutching her little boy's hand, sobbing, and looking beseechingly upward. "Tommy, I've lost my courage. I don't know what else to do. I'm so afraid!"

Tom held her. "Darling, I want you to go home. You need to rest. I'll stay here with Nicholas. We have to trust the doctors. They say the antibiotics will knock it out."

"I know, I know. But he looks so *bad,* and he's hurting. Why can't they give him more pain medicine?"

Jayne went home and lay down. That night her father called for the daily update.

"How are things, kiddo?"

That's all it took. Jayne opened up. She sobbed and screamed and questioned, over and over: Why us? Why Nicholas? Why was it happening? Why had she lost courage? Her father responded gently, and for the next hour they had a healing father-daughter talk.

But the anger persisted. The next morning, as we walked through the lobby on the way to the escalators, a nondescript doctor in a lab coat walked by us. Jayne turned to Tom and said, "You know, I've never seen that doctor before in my life, but I hate him. I could lash out and kick him."

"I know the feeling," Tom said.

"It's just that he represents this hospital—the control it has over our lives and Nicholas. I should be grateful. I *know* I should be grateful, but it's hard when Nicholas is suffering so much obvious pain. He's just an innocent baby. He doesn't deserve *this* on top of everything else. I just want to take his pain away and make him stop hurting."

Jayne shook white-knuckled fists at the institution around us. In another minute, she sighed, then said, "Tom, I think I'm finally cracking up. Why should I want to harm that doctor? He's probably a very nice man who's never even seen Nicholas."

"You just said it," Tom said. "We're tired, and we have *no* control over anything right now. We just want to be out of here, but we can't, and that doctor symbolizes everything we need to get away from. I know; I feel it, too."

It was a strain to keep our anger in check and our faces and voices masked, but somehow we managed it—more for Nicholas' sake than anything else.

᭣

The antibiotics quickly stopped the peritoneal infection, and by March 15, Nicholas' one-month birthday, dialysis was discontinued altogether and the tube removed from his abdomen.

On this momentous day, we felt so buoyed that we mailed his birth announcements and brought lollipops tied with little blue ribbons to all the ICN staff. Lionel Richie and Jayne sang a duet, and in fact we *did* have a party . . . at least, a miniparty—as much as we could in isolation! The nurses on the night shift did their own celebrating. One brought him a balloon, another made a colorful, custom-designed "Nicholas" sign for his crib, and Mary gave him a little blue rattle that looked like a barbell and a small stuffed Odie, which in days to come would often have a nipple taped to its nose for a pacifier.

Then the breathing tube came out on March 17. Little Kyle, with the help of his mom, sent Nicholas a St. Patrick's Day card to celebrate. We were almost giddy with happiness. We actually saw our son's lips again, and his tongue.

Yet it was the oddest thing; he cried, but he made no sound. His vocal cords, still swollen from the breathing tube that had been wedged between them all those weeks, simply didn't function. It was terribly touching. Our baby wailed "at the top of his lungs," yet not the slightest sound emerged.

Three days later, on March 20, we were allowed to hold him for the first time in four weeks. Just to hold his soft little body in our arms again after his having survived impossible odds was both a joy and an affirmation of so much we believed in. We would've preferred not to wear our plastic gloves, of course, but as the nurses bundled him in blankets and carefully handed him to us— for he still had a number of IV tubes and monitor wires attached— we were without doubt the proudest parents alive!

Fussy at first, Nicholas finally relaxed, sucked down half an ounce of formula from his mom, and burped twice. Tom beamed as he once again took his son from Jayne. Someone pushed a rocking chair into the isolation area and we took turns contentedly feeding and rocking our boy.

Later in the afternoon, a meeting was convened by the chief neonatologist, Dr. Sunshine, who had worked in the ICN for over twenty years. All of Nicholas' primary doctors, nurses, and social workers assembled, along with ourselves, in the conference room. The purpose of the meeting was to provide us with a summary of what Nicholas had been through and an up-to-date prognosis.

We were told that they'd finally grown a virus out of the cultures that had been started weeks before. It was of the enterovirus family, probably a coxsackie virus—a common virus that in a normal person would have manifested itself as a sore throat and a cold. In Nicholas, who probably picked it up in utero and whose immune system for some unknown reason hadn't attacked it, the virus had waged a war that ravaged nearly every major organ in his body. Any one of the illnesses and resulting crises he had had could have been—indeed, *should* have been—fatal. The hospital staff had done its best to buy Nicholas time while what they thought was a virus ran its course.

At the time of this meeting, it seemed they had succeeded. There were no longer any signs of the infection, and—wondrously!— nearly all the affected organs seemed to have recovered, probably due to Nicholas' youth and the resilience of his tissue. Nevertheless, his heart muscle, that of the left ventricle in particular, had been severely damaged, with the result that the rest of his heart had to work especially hard and, because of this, had enlarged. Other organs could frequently heal and become as good as new; heart tissue could not.

Nicholas' heartbeat was dangerously irregular, but he still responded well to lidocaine. So well, in fact, that there really was only one hurdle remaining before we could take our son home: a substitute for lidocaine had to be found—something we could give him orally, since obviously we couldn't take home a new baby attached to an IV pump.

Still, Dr. Sunshine explained, even when they hit upon the right oral medication and we took him home, there were three possible future scenarios: First, as Nicholas grew older, his body would grow around his enlarged heart, which could also improve somewhat; though he wouldn't be completely healed, he could live a comparatively normal life. Second, his heart could weaken over a period of years and eventually fail altogether. Third, his heart might simply fail unexpectedly, and soon.

The last was a worst-case situation, the doctor emphasized, and with a beaming smile to match his name, he said, "All in all, your son has turned out to be an AFM."

"Dr. Sunshine," Tom asked, drained by the deluge of data we'd just received, "*What* is an AFM?"

Still beaming, the doctor looked at us both, tapped his pen on the table, and said—and these are his exact words—"Why, he's another friggin' miracle!" Then, after a long pause: "Despite everything we did and are doing for Nicholas, we can't claim him. He's not a medical miracle. We don't know why he survived. He simply shouldn't have. The fact that he's still with us has got to be chalked up as a real miracle."

Chapter Six

We bundled Nicholas in a fluffy white blanket and securely strapped him into his car seat. Jayne got into the back seat with him, and Tom pulled away from Stanford Hospital's curb.

"Can you believe we're finally going home?" Tom asked. "It seems as if we've lived in that hospital since the dawn of time. I feel like we've been reborn!"

"The whole experience seems so . . . unbelievable," Jayne answered, gazing down at our swaddled son. "You're a real-life hero, Nicholas, and we're proud of you."

Happy silence replaced conversation as Jayne adjusted Nicholas' blanket and stroked his cheeks. Tom cherished these simple and tender actions in the rearview mirror. During the twenty-mile drive on the freeway, he thought, *I don't know how we did it, but somehow we got through Hell together.* He watched his wife and son and remembered the long month that had followed Nicholas' achieving "miracle" status.

The evening following Dr. Sunshine's announcement, Jayne had sat down at her polished oak desk to pen a six-page letter in tiny script to the mother of the one-year-old we'd been considering adopting. ". . . And we told the doctors today about Gabriel. They warned us firmly that Nicholas must be kept away from people with illnesses—especially children, who are prone to colds and infections. . . ." It hurt, but we had to pass on that chance.

As he drove up Interstate 280, on his left Tom saw Crystal Springs Reservoir sparkling in the late-morning sun. The bright, dancing pinpoints of light seemed to keep time with his happy memories: with the big and little triumphs—of dressing our son for the first time in the outfit Jayne had kept in her car for so long, of his voice returning by increments, of his discovering his hands, of his eyes following a mobile around and around, of his first tub bath. . . .

After numerous frustrating failures, an exhaustive search of the medical literature, and calls to colleagues throughout the country, Nicholas' doctors had finally found a substitute for lidocaine. A doctor on the East Coast claimed success controlling arrhythmias in two- and three-year-olds with *oral* doses of a potent IV solution—quinidine gluconate—mixed with cherry syrup. Using this recipe, the Stanford pharmacy mixed up a batch, and at last Nicholas' heartbeat held steady! But this nationwide search hammered home a vital point: *No one at all had experience controlling arrhythmias in a baby of Nicholas' age.* Truly our little boy was breaking new ground!

. . . The sign up ahead announced our exit. Home lay just a turn-off away. The home we'd prayed we'd bring Nicholas to—*our family home.* Tom saw Jayne's head resting on the back of the seat, her eyes closed. He swelled with pride. She'd been so brave—stronger than he'd ever imagined possible.

The last four days in the hospital had been a whirlwind. Nicholas' last IV was removed. We practiced CPR, rented a home heart monitor, received lessons in dispensing medications, and packed his many toys, gifts, and supplies.

Then the day we'd been waiting for dawned gloriously—the day that the doctors had said they'd discharge Nicholas. We arrived at the hospital full of gleeful anticipation. Refusing to wear plastic gloves, Jayne dressed Nicholas in a cheerful red suit, and our son felt the touch of his mother's real hands again for the first time in two months.

Yet even with our hopes up so high, the doctors weren't in complete accord. One was emphatic: "Nicky," he said (as we winced at the nickname), "is certainly better. But he's still having nearly 300 irregular beats an hour. You're premature in thinking we'll discharge him today." But he must have seen the pleading in our eyes. The doctors conferred yet again. In the end, one cardiologist broke away from the group and strode purposefully over to us.

"Good news," she said, with a broad smile. "You can take Nicholas home."

We pulled into the country court that our log house shared with five others in a woodsy setting. As we rolled into our driveway, we saw our neighbor Jan sweeping leaves in front of her house. We got out of the car, and Tom yelled up the court, "Jan, Nicholas is with us. He's come home!" Jan, who'd had a running summary of events during the preceding nine weeks, threw down her broom and rushed to meet us as we hurried to get Nicholas indoors.

Jayne held Nicholas as we rushed up the concrete stairs of our house. Tom pushed the front door open—and his wife and son entered. Upon crossing the threshold, Jayne felt Nicholas immediately relax. In months to come, she would often describe it: "As soon as we walked in, and Nicholas saw our colorful little house and looked out the windows at all the green trees, I could feel him *untense* in my arms; he visibly relaxed. It was the most extraordinary feeling—like 'Oh, Mommy, I *like* it here.' "

Once inside, Tom said to Jan, "Do you realize that you have the distinction of being the first person Nicholas has met outside of a hospital?"

"Really? Great! Isn't he gorgeous! Oh, I want to hold him."

Tom asked her to wash her hands. When she had, she gently took our little boy into her arms. "He's so little!" she exclaimed, looking at him fondly. Nicholas, in his turn, studied Jan intently. His eyes roved over her youthful tan features, shoulder-length rich brown hair, and paisley sweatshirt. She stayed about a half-hour, and then we were alone with our little boy for the first time in our home—indeed, for the first time in nine weeks. The bassinet stood in the nursery, its blue skirting and ruffles freshly starched and pressed. We snuggled "our little prince" down into it and covered him cozily with blankets.

Then the realization hit us: we had our lives back! The feeling was glorious. As Nicholas napped, we luxuriated in spending an afternoon at home without "life and death" pressures constantly hanging over our heads. There was none of the tension of "we really must get back to the hospital" that had been our constant companion when we weren't at Nicholas' side. Now we were all home together, relaxed and happy and grateful beyond words that we'd all survived against the odds!

We unpacked the bags of medications that we had brought home and organized them in a kitchen cupboard. Then we prepared checklists that noted the times (every four hours) and dosages for the *seven* different meds Nicholas required. Soon enough we learned that these forms were critical; keeping track of who had given what when would have been impossible without them.

We carefully drew his medicines into calibrated blue-and-white plastic oral syringes and squirted measured amounts into his formula to disguise their bitterness. These syringes, which looked like hypodermic syringes without needles, became a ubiquitous part of our lives. In short order, they were everywhere—in the kitchen, diaper bag, nursery, and glove compartment—all drawn-up and ready to go, or being washed or dried. If there were "uninitiated" people around when the time came for Nicholas' next dose—whether we had guests at home or were out on a shopping expedition—you'd think from their expressions when we pulled out as many as five syringes that we were mad scientists about to torture the child!

Immediately our lives settled down into a blessed pattern. Jayne was on maternity leave, and Tom stayed home for the first week to help his family settle in.

Because Nicholas' normal development had been in a very true sense "on hold" for nine weeks, he was practically a newborn—8 pounds, 2 ounces—when we brought him home. We had to remember, therefore, when we put him down for a nap or at night, to keep him on his side with a tightly rolled blanket under his back. This was to prevent him from rolling onto his back and possibly inhaling saliva or vomit, or rolling onto his stomach and smothering. Because of his damaged heart, one unshakable fear was always with us; we lived *every day of his life* with the dread of checking him at naptime and finding that he'd stopped breathing. Though we both had had CPR training, and despite all the joy we shared and the apparent improvement of Nicholas' condition, this particular fear never varied, never lessened.

For the first few months, we rented a heart monitor to use at home. Twice a day we would apply a Velcro belt across our son's chest and record his heart rhythm on a strip of chart paper. If we observed anything unusual, we were to call Dr. Rubenstein. We also took his pulse regularly before giving him his medicines. We quickly became comfortable with these rituals, and Nicholas accepted them all with panache.

Soon one concern we'd harbored for weeks was laid to rest. It had occurred to us that because Nicholas had spent the first weeks of his life not only under bright lights twenty-four hours a day, but surrounded with the hubbub of a noisy hospital ward, perhaps the quiet and dark of his nursery at night would be uncomfortable for him. But Nicholas loved peace and quiet and relative darkness.

At that time we kept a night light on, if for no other reason than so Tom could see where he was going in the middle of the night when he got up to give his son his two o'clock quinidine. After a few days, Tom needed to set three alarm clocks to ensure that he would awaken. After he slept through all three alarms one time— and realizing that our medication schedule was merely a holdover from a hospital routine that didn't differentiate between day and night—we adjusted the entire schedule back one hour; the night meds now fell at nine and one, which was a little better. If Tom could just stay up until one every night, he wouldn't need to awaken until five, which was when he would normally get up to go to work. But then, staying up until one every night began to have its drawbacks, too. It took a few months, but, by trial and error, giving Nicholas his night meds settled into a comfortable routine.

Mornings generally began, after Daddy left for work, with a bottle followed by playtime. Jayne played records with upbeat tunes and happy singing, such as the soundtrack albums from *The*

Sound of Music and *The Muppet Movie*. Nicholas responded to the cheerful sounds and many different voices that filled the house. In the afternoons, Jayne frequently played *Fiddler on the Roof,* and Nicholas seemed to look around for Daddy when he heard Tevye's deep tones.

Another important part of each day was exercise time. Nicholas needed help to flex and loosen his limbs and to encourage head control. Because he'd spent so much time restrained in the hospital, his neck muscles were weak and his head floppy. Jayne placed him on his tummy on the couch with a colorful toy or his bottle a short distance in front of and above him, then coached him to look up at them. She also laid him on his back and played with toys and rattles above his head, encouraging him to reach his arms up purposefully. Very quickly he developed a happy, smiling personality.

Another favorite pastime began for medicinal reasons, then developed into a delightful game. At one point, Nicholas developed a diaper rash, and Jayne had the idea of laying our son on a colorful quilt in the middle of the living room floor, where each morning a sunbeam shone through the window. She placed Nicholas on his tummy with a diaper under him and his bare bottom in the middle of the bright beam—usurping Kipling's favorite spot! Nicholas loved it. The warmth tickled him, and he was all smiles as he exercised and played. His rash quickly disappeared, too! We called this "sunbeam therapy," and it became part of his morning playtime.

While basking in the sunbeam, Nicholas loved to kick. This and the fact that his legs were long and skinny brought to mind Kermit the Frog; so, for a while, Nicholas was known as Kermee. When Jayne called him that, imitating the falsetto voice of Miss Piggy, his giggles were inevitable and contagious. Our little boy was growing and happy—smiles were plentiful, and we were delighted to enjoy a real infancy stage with him even though he was now three months old.

During these first few weeks at home, Nicholas had many visitors. We screened them for any symptoms of illness, of course, explaining Nicholas' susceptibility to infection. He gained weight steadily and grew quickly. We had weekly appointments at the cardiology clinic at Stanford, and we saw Dr. Rubenstein regularly. In addition, Nicholas had monthly physical therapy assessments at Stanford to monitor his motor development and coordination.

After he'd been home about a month, we took Nicholas to church for the first time. Our friend Fr. Miles Riley (whose invitation to Jayne to watch the taping of his TV talk show was the catalyst of our meeting) was assigned to St. Gabriel's Church in San Francisco, and we wanted to introduce him to Nicholas. Our son was alert and quiet throughout the celebration. He responded to the music and to Miles' booming, theatrical, passionately sincere homily by looking around and smiling. We took turns holding him on our shoulders, and the people in the pew behind us whispered, "Isn't he cute!" "Dear, he's looking at me!" "What a *precious* little one." Afterwards Nicholas got to meet Miles. All and all, our son's first real outing was a rousing success.

Our adoption paperwork had been filed early on by our attorney. In mid May, we had our first home-study evaluation by the county social worker assigned to our case. Tom took the morning off, and we had a long interview. The social worker proved to be very pleasant. She was interested in our relationships with our parents and each other. We spoke about child care, and she asked how we anticipated that we'd share with Nicholas the fact that he was adopted.

"Actually, Rosemary," Tom said, "we don't foresee any problem with that. We know the school of thought used to be to avoid telling the child. But that almost always ended in the child's finding out accidentally—with a major family crisis resulting. And then the child could well develop identity problems. We've heard of cases of adopted children becoming obsessed with trying to find their real parents—some spending a good portion of their adult lives in the search."

Jayne continued: "Our plan is never to treat the word *adopt* any differently than any other word, and never to hide the fact of adoption. Basically, Nicholas will grow up taking for granted that he's adopted. Should he choose to seek out his birthparents, we'll help him as much as we can."

"Fine," said Rosemary. "Studies *do* show that candidness from the start is best. Tell me—how would you answer if Nicholas asked you *why* he was adopted?"

"We'd tell him that his birthmother loved him so much that she wanted the very best for him, which she knew she wouldn't be able to provide. And we adopted him into our family because from the first second we saw him, we loved him—a feeling that only grew in intensity with each passing day. Let's face it, Rosemary: Nicholas is not your ordinary child. Thank God, you wouldn't know he was sick by looking at him, but he requires—and has required from day one—a lot of special attention. We're just grateful that God chose us to be his parents."

Before she left, Rosemary explained that a subsequent interview would be needed before the final recommendation could be sent to the judge. She also told us that all children adopted through the county agency were automatically covered by MediCal (California's state medical coverage), but because Nicholas was being adopted privately, he wasn't eligible.

"That doesn't seem right," Tom said. "The agency is handling the adoption paperwork and authorization anyway. The fact that he didn't originally come through the agency is just a technicality."

"Nevertheless, the law is quite clear in the matter, Mr. Miller."

Not wanting to press the issue, we made a tentative appointment for a follow-up interview.

◄§

By mid June, Nicholas had learned to hold his own bottle. This *major feat* made Nicholas independent, and suddenly we each had both of our hands free again. He also began playing vigorously with small toys and rattles and especially enjoyed holding them above his head for minutes at a time. Even if he didn't have anything in his hands, he'd stare at them, enraptured, turning them over slowly and examining them as though he were thinking, *Look at these wonderful things. I wonder what they're for. Hey, I can wiggle my fingers!*

About this time, he also learned to turn over from his back to his tummy and repeated this trick several times each day. To think that such a simple feat could thrill his parents so! We were proud of *each* of our son's achievements. After having gone through so much, he was growing and developing just as the baby books said he should. He just tended to be a couple of months late.

It was at this time that Dr. Rubenstein gave us the go-ahead on adding solid foods to his diet. We started with rice cereal, which was not appreciated. The faces he made were priceless; we kept a camera close during mealtimes and took many a memorable snapshot.

Nicholas enjoyed car travel. He chortled and giggled and jabbered aloud on outings. Errands were a joy with such a willing companion. Jayne stocked the diaper bag, then placed Nicholas wide-eyed in his car seat on the front seat facing the back so that she could instantly assess him. As she drove, she talked to Nicholas animatedly.

"Daddy's off at work, little guy, making books about computers that you'll read someday and I'll *never* understand." Jayne chuckled aloud and Nicholas grinned, as if he knew just how funny this really was.

Nicholas was very portable and amazingly adaptable. Jayne zipped him out of the car and into the cleaners, back to the car, over to the market—and he was nearly always happy and alert to the adventure of it all. The supermarket was clearly his favorite—so many colorful cans and boxes aisle after aisle.

"Let's see now, Nicholas. We need grapefruit juice and cranberry juice, and here's the soup for Daddy's favorite chicken and rice casserole. How about some apricots for you, my son? Are they still your favorite?"

The produce aisle was yet another adventure. Jayne picked and squeezed and called out the names and colors of her choices: *"Green* broccoli and *red* peppers for a little boy named Nicholas. Bananas are *yellow,* and you love bananas. Should we get a whole bunch for a little monkey like you?" And then she'd tickle his tummy.

Nicholas was truly a buddy and thrived on the interaction and the fun he had with Mommy. An extrovert, and never one to miss a trick, he looked around at people constantly. And people were attracted to him. "Well, hello there, young man—aren't you a handsome little boy." Jayne would look up from ferreting out a bargain and smile. Nicholas' newest fan would then offer totally unsolicited advice on parenting and launch into a story about how quickly his or her own children had grown, cautioning Jayne to appreciate this "cute" stage, as all too soon "they become little monsters."

Once when all three of us were at the market perusing the meat section, choosing chicken to barbecue that evening, an elderly gentleman materialized beside our basket. "Do you both realize," he said, "that the first year in a child's life is his most important?"

We looked around and winked subtly at one another. Jayne could read Tom's mind: *So this is how it happens!*

We thanked him and tried to continue our shopping, but the man wouldn't have it. "I've just read an article . . . ," he continued. When finally he relented and we were able to move on, Tom wondered aloud: "Does this sort of thing happen to other parents? Or does Nicholas somehow attract it? Is this charisma in action?" Regardless of the explanation, there was no doubt that Nicholas simply caught people's eyes—and perhaps their hearts—the instant they saw him.

But there was another aspect to errand-running that Jayne didn't enjoy: encountering parents and children "locked in battle." She felt wrenched inside at the sadness of it. Seeing a youngster's arm yanked and hearing loud admonitions of "If you don't put that back, I'm going to smack you" or "Go ahead and cry; I don't care" always tugged at Jayne's own heart. After all we'd been through—after being shown early on how very fragile life could be—Jayne simply couldn't understand these scenes.

Not wanting Nicholas exposed to this negative energy, she always moved quickly to another area of the store. Nicholas had thrived under consistent nurture and discipline. "No" meant "no," and he understood that. We made a concerted effort not to let our own exhaustion, fatigue, and frustration control us when Nicholas became fussy and demanding. Usually it was as simple as taking several deep breaths and saying, "I know you're tired and fussy, Nicholas, and so is Mommy. As soon as we get home, we're both going to have some cold apple juice and take our naps. How 'bout it, little buddy?" For him, a nuzzle and cuddle were much more calming than being screamed at and yanked around.

We were very blessed. Nicholas had an easily consolable nature that thrived on positive attention. We knew he trusted us, and he knew we loved him unconditionally. This was the bedrock of our family dynamic and enriched our experiences together each day. We simply included Nicholas in the "couple experience" we had nurtured since our engagement seven years before. We respected, trusted, and loved one another, and our relationship with our child was an outgrowth of this same experience.

In late June, Nicholas had an appointment with Dr. Roger Winkle, a young cardiologist who specialized in arrhythmias. He had seen Nicholas at Stanford during our son's final weeks there. Pleased with Nicholas' progress, and hearing for himself that Nicholas' heart sounds were effectively normal, he decided it was time to discontinue the quinidine. To do this, however, he wanted to put Nicholas back in the hospital to monitor how his heart reacted to the change. During the twenty-four hours prior to Nicholas' return to the hospital, he wore a portable heart monitor—like a small tape recorder with wires taped to his chest—to determine his heart rate for a full day on the regular dose of quinidine.

When processed through a computer, the tape produced an

electrocardiogram tracing that showed that Nicholas had had only fifty-seven irregular heartbeats during that time. We were elated, as were doctors Winkle and Rubenstein. Fifty-seven PVCs (as some arrhythmias are called) during a day were considered essentially normal. This was in comparison to about 300 *an hour* when we brought him home from Stanford.

Dr. Winkle then admitted Nicholas to the Pediatric ICU at Stanford, and the quinidine was discontinued. As his last dose wore off, we could clearly see on the room heart monitor that Nicholas' arrhythmias were increasing. Not only were they increasing, but they frequently doubled and even tripled up, which is a bad sign. The bunching up of PVCs frequently leads to fibrillation; the heart's regular pattern is disrupted, potentially causing cardiac arrest. The longer we watched, the more uneasy we became.

The irony of all this was that Nicholas was having a great time! He didn't look as though he had a severe heart problem. He smiled impishly and giggled and played with his toys. His olive coloring was normal. There didn't appear to be a thing wrong with him. In fact, we got some odd looks from the other visitors in the intensive care ward, as if to say, "What on earth is *he* doing in here? Why is he taking up valuable bedspace? My child is deathly ill. Go home where you belong." Yet, despite Nicholas' cheerfulness, his monitor belied appearances.

During the evening of the second day, we were sitting with Nicholas when the results of the first day's tracing were phoned in. Nicholas had had more than 7,000 PVCs in those twenty-four hours! Dr. Winkle immediately ordered Nicholas back on his quinidine. We were disappointed and more than a little frightened. Despite appearances, Nicholas' heart hadn't yet healed appreciably. But as the quinidine took effect, there was also a feeling of relief that the one hard-fought-for medication that kept his heart beating regularly was still effective.

Afterwards we'd often catch ourselves looking with awe at the plain brown pharmaceutical bottle containing the cherry-tinged, quinine-bitter solution. Its refrigerated contents were keeping our boy alive.

Nicholas stayed in the hospital for another day under observation. His heart settled down to a normal rhythm quickly. That evening, as he slept peacefully in Jayne's arms, we pondered aloud the dread consequences of his being attacked by a simple virus.

"I just don't understand it," Tom said quietly. "His birthmom didn't have any prenatal care, but that doesn't explain why he got so sick. She said she'd had a cold a couple of days before she gave birth. But that doesn't explain it either. I'm sure babies are born all the time from moms with colds, and *they* don't get sick—or if they do, they catch a cold. Big deal."

"You know, darling," Jayne responded. "Nicholas' symptoms came on much too fast for him to have caught the virus at birth. He must have somehow picked it up in utero."

"But the same point holds. Why doesn't every baby born of a mom with a cold get as sick as Nicholas? Why didn't Nicholas' immune system kick on and fight it off?"

"I don't know," Jayne said, cuddling her little boy closer, lovingly studying every curve in his innocent face. "I don't think anybody knows. That's part of the problem."

Tom was quiet for a few minutes, then spoke again. "There are studies showing that a person is more likely to get sick if depressed. Depression, sadness, feelings of hopelessness somehow suppress the immune system. Do you think Nicholas could have felt his mom's vibes—'I don't want you. Why'd you have to happen to me? I'm giving you away'—with the effect that his immune system simply didn't bother to fight the virus?"

Jayne looked at Tom with interest. "You know, that may have contributed to it. She may have felt he was a big imposition and just wanted to be rid of him. Take the fact that she didn't have any prenatal care. And yet she didn't have an abortion—thank God! That would've been the easiest way out for her. I suppose her respect for life was too great, or something, to go that far. Yet she couldn't bring herself to want or love him. And in not wanting him, she unknowingly made him vulnerable. So vulnerable that he caught the virus that had given her a cold, and—"

Jayne wasn't able to finish the sentence. Tears welled in her eyes as she remembered what we'd been through and the damaged heart Nicholas was left with as the legacy of it all. Tom knew her thoughts well, for they were his, too. *It just isn't fair. It just isn't fair.*

Though we would never have any proof, after this whispered discussion in yet another hospital intensive care ward, we never doubted that we'd hit on the most likely explanation. How many times since then have we wondered, *If only she'd loved him a little bit more . . . ?*

(Letting her child be born . . . and then caring enough to want him to be adopted by a good family had to be considered a loving gesture. Yet she seemed to have forgotten that *nurturing* him through his first nine months of life was a vital part of that gesture.)

܍

The next morning, as we got Nicholas packed and ready to leave, the results of the second day's tracings, recorded before the quinidine was readministered, came in. Unbelievably, he'd had over 12,000 PVCs during the second twenty-four-hour period! This meant that our son could be in a life-threatening medical situation—virtually knocking on death's door—and we wouldn't know it by looking at him; his activity level and general appearance might well remain normal, as demonstrated in the previous two days. It was a frightening realization. Nevertheless, the doctor told us there was still an even chance that as Nicholas grew, his body could grow around his enlarged heart, stabilizing his condition.

Back at home, our daily routine quickly returned. Because Tom's vacation in February hadn't really been a vacation at all— only the most hair-raising time of his entire life!—he arranged things at his office to take another week off in late June. After all, he still had that mystery novel to finish writing, and he could do it only if he had a chunk of uninterrupted time.

This time his vacation began in the middle of the week. He'd been home only a day (just a week after Nicholas' second homecoming from Stanford) when the phone rang.

"Hi, Tom. This is Allan." It was Tom's boss' boss, the vice-president of marketing. "Have you heard about the reorganization at the office?"

"No—" *Now why on earth is he calling me on my vacation?* Tom wondered.

"Well, as you know, our Japanese vendor is having problems delivering parts for our new computer. Despite the fact that we have thousands of orders, we don't have nearly enough product to ship, which means that our projected income for the next couple of quarters will be severely reduced. We can get enough venture capital to keep us afloat, however. But there is one catch. The people who have the money will help us out only if we show that we can cut our expenses by two million dollars. What that means is that we've cut back throughout the company. There are thirty-nine people affected in marketing, including the entire publications department."

Despite the barrage of euphemisms, Tom couldn't believe what he'd just heard.

"Excuse me, Allan, are you saying that, as of now, there is *no publications department?*"

"Yes."

"That means I no longer have a job."

"That's true."

Tom cupped the receiver and looked at Jayne, who was sitting close by, waiting impatiently. "I've just been laid off."

"No!" Jayne covered her face with her hands.

"I'm sorry, Tom, that you had to find out this way. We had a general meeting this morning to make the announcement. You were the only one not there. Can you come in tomorrow to clean out your desk?"

Chapter Seven

The next morning, while Tom boxed up his personal effects at the office and said farewell to his workmates, Jayne contacted California Children's Services (CCS) again. One realization had hit home immediately: we were about to lose Tom's insurance—which had covered much of Nicholas' hospitalization and which ordinarily would have continued to give our son blanket health coverage. Now, because he had a "preexisting condition," no insurance company would cover him. Jayne informed CCS of the abrupt decrease in our income and asked if we could be reevaluated. The agency representative said she'd look into it.

When Tom came home, he had under his arm copies of the latest editions of four local newspapers. As he pored over the classified sections, ripping out various help-wanted ads, he suddenly looked up. "Jayne, I just had a horrible thought. What if this affects the adoption? Our income has been halved. Oh, my God!"

During the next few days, as we cared for our son, many concerns and fears tumbled through our minds. But we had no idea that Tom's being laid off would actually be a blessing in disguise—for two reasons. The first became apparent very quickly. Two days after Jayne had called CCS, the phone rang.

"Hello, Mrs. Miller. This is Sue at CCS. I have good and bad news for you. The good news is that Nicholas will be covered from now on by CCS, not because your husband's been laid off, but because Nicholas is adopted. The bad news is that he should've been covered all along. When I was looking into your new circumstances, I discovered that adopted children with qualifying illnesses are immediately eligible, regardless of family income. I have to apologize to you. Nicholas was eligible from the start, and we made a mistake turning you down because of your income."

Jayne was thrilled. "Sue, I must say, you've really made my day.

What do we need to do now to defray the large outstanding debt at Stanford?"

"All bills and copies of insurance payments should be forwarded to our office. We'll cover most of the outstanding debt retroactively, starting from the day you were referred to our office. All of his bills for the first two weeks remain your responsibility, however."

Jayne set about compiling the necessary data. Nicholas' initial computer-generated Stanford bill was half an inch thick, and the unfolded pages of fanfold paper could stretch the length of our house and back again. This initial bill ran well into six figures! Still, several times a week additional bills arrived in the mail as they were processed. But from this point on, CCS covered all heart-related medical care that Nicholas received.

The second blessing to come from Tom's no longer having a nine-to-six job took us longer to recognize. Despite his spending hours responding to ads, and interviewing, and freelancing on temporary projects, *Tom was at home most of the time and able to spend that time with Nicholas.* It was a chance that many new fathers don't ever have. And once it hit home, we realized what a wonderful opportunity had been presented to us.

"Who would've thought," Jayne said one day, "that losing your job could be such a positive experience—at least in some ways?"

"I guess it's a twist of fate that we should be grateful for," Tom said, "but it's really made me think. There are so many new dads out there who don't even know what they're missing. They have no clue. Somehow they have to learn. They've got to understand that spending time with their children when they're babies is a priceless opportunity. A lot of them might say, 'That's women's work.' Bull! I suppose others of them say, 'There's plenty of time. We'll go to the ball game later on.' But that's the point. *Later on* is a long time off, and by then they've missed so much that's important in that child's life. And then they wonder why they don't get along with their kids!"

For the remainder of summer and through early fall, the Miller family was together. Though freelance work provided steady income, we were naturally concerned about Tom's finding permanent work—not only for its own sake but to head off any possibility of the adoption going wrong. Yet those months together were priceless. Tom was able to bond with Nicholas and *watch* him develop instead of merely hearing about his little triumphs at the end of an exhausting day at the office and an even worse commute—when everybody's energy was at an ebb, and fussiness the order of the hour.

Certainly Nicholas' fussy time was early evening. Every night around seven, he'd become agitated and start to cry for no apparent reason. Despite all his needs having been taken care of, almost nothing calmed him down. At first confused and worried, we checked child-care books and read articles in *Parents* magazine and the like, only to discover that our son's mood shifts in the evening were perfectly normal.

However, his crankiness still needed attention. Finally, by trial and error, we hit on the one thing that quickly calmed him down. He loved to be walked—especially by Daddy. Tom would hold him in his arms and pace the living room, then walk throughout our small house, sometimes for hours. Despite his love for Nicholas, and the dear feeling of tightly holding his warm little boy, the pacing grew very old *very* quickly. Tom tried watching TV, but usually there was nothing on that interested him. We solved this problem by simply renting movies. By pacing with the TV and VCR on, both of Jayne's fellows were able to carry on, and Jayne could get some rest. This phase, thank goodness, lasted only a few months.

Jayne returned to her job in mid July, working two or three swing shifts each week. Tom was able to arrange to bring his freelance work home, and to have his interviews in the morning, so that he could be with his son when Jayne worked. Since Nicholas had usually had his nap by the time Jayne left at two, Tom and Nicholas spent most of their time together in the living room, where a large blanket had been spread on the floor so Nicholas could have a clean surface to play on.

At this time, he was learning to get from point A to point B by rocking his little body, rolling over, grunting, getting toeholds on a wrinkle in the blanket, and pushing himself forward. It wasn't official creeping, and certainly far from crawling, but it was amazing to see the determination with which he maneuvered himself around. He'd get a set look in his eyes, and by God he'd get to his destination—which was usually Kipling contentedly minding his business on a corner of the blanket in his favorite sunbeam—if it was the last thing he did! Kipling, for his part, watched all this with the jaundiced eye of experience. Nicholas was *fascinated* by his cat, who seemed to give him a reason to stretch out his seeking hands. Frequently Kipling was too comfortable to move, despite our son's having docked alongside. Then Nicholas would grab a handful of fur and tug for all he was worth, stretching the loose skin in all directions as if it were taffy. Instinctively Kipling seemed to understand that Nicholas didn't mean anything by it. When he got bored with being mauled, or his feline patience came to an end, he'd stand royally, stretch lingeringly, shake briskly, and jump onto the bookshelf or go off for a snack.

Afternoons passed quickly as Tom roughhoused with his son, threw him in the air, rolled around with him on the floor, and made a Big Issue of playing "Bring Back the Toy" when Nicholas nonchalantly tossed one aside. This always provoked a delightful chorus of infectious baby giggles. With Jayne away at work, Tom not only played and exercised with Nicholas, but made tickling games out of changing diapers, airplane games out of mealtimes, and generally took care of all his son's needs.

As Nicholas' parents, we made a point of treating Nicholas normally. It was a conscious value judgment we'd discussed months earlier with Dr. Rubenstein. We had decided that, if Nicholas had any chance at all of growing into a self-confident, productive adult, we couldn't allow ourselves to treat him like a China doll—which was the big temptation. Laurie listened to our feelings on the matter and wholeheartedly affirmed our policy. "You guys sound as if you have it together. Just remember—there are legitimate times to be cautious. He's not a cast-iron football."

Along these lines, we refused to buy into other people's expectations. They assumed that because Nicholas had been so sick, he must be especially frail. Many acquaintances were shocked to see us treat him as though he were a perfectly healthy and normal little boy.

"Shouldn't you be more careful with him?" they'd ask.

Our answer was simple: "And have him grow up to think he could get away with murder just because he has a heart problem? It's critical that Nicholas' health history *not be used as an excuse by him.* And this has got to begin now. Besides, look at him. Does he look like a sickly child to you?"

Then we'd explain that the only concessions we made to his medical problems were keeping him away from people who were obviously ill and being punctual with his medications, responsibilities that had become second nature.

One day in early August, Rosemary, our adoption social worker, called us with some important news. She repeated that, though Nicholas was now covered by CCS, he was denied MediCal coverage for non-heart-related problems—a fact that had given us much anxiety. She went on to say, however, that she'd just heard about another couple whose child had been denied MediCal for reasons similar to ours; they had sued the state of California and won. Though this was an isolated incident, it did create a precedent. Perhaps our attorney might be able to look into the matter on our behalf. We thanked Rosemary and immediately called Diane. She explained that she hadn't yet heard of the specific case Rosemary had referred to, but she'd look into it right away.

Diane knew, of course, that agency-adopted children were automatically put on state health coverage; privately adopted children were not. We agreed that there definitely was a bias in "the adoption game": social workers were typically pro-agency, probably because they had far less control over private placement, in which parental evaluation is done only after the child is home.

Jayne holding her three-hour-old son, Nicholas, for the first time, February 15, 1985.

For three weeks, while attached to a respirator, Nicholas's life hung by a thread in Stanford Hospital's Intensive Care Nursery.

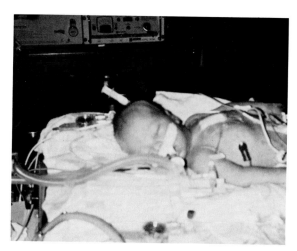

Tom and Jayne, with nine-week-old Nicholas, smile for the Stanford Hospital staff before taking Nicholas home, April 19, 1985.

Katie and Nicholas.

Nicholas and Tom at home near the
books Nicholas loved to scatter over
the floor in their San Francisco
Peninsula home.

We dressed Nicholas as a clown for
Halloween 1985.

Nicholas Lawrence Miller is officially adopted on
December 4, 1985. He is shown here with his proud
parents and the county judge.

Nine-month portrait.

Four-month portrait.

One-year portrait.

Nicholas gives his mom and dad a big smile. *Courtesy R. Portillo, LLUMC Audio-Visual Services.*

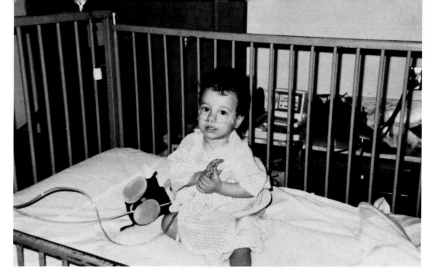

Nicholas in District Hospital on April 7, 1986, battling pneumonia and congestive heart failure.

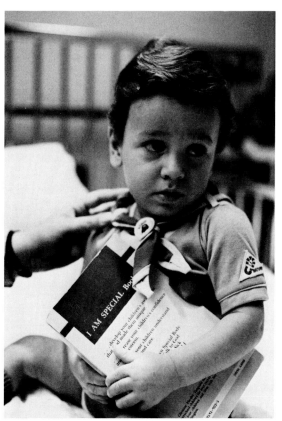

A serious moment before Nicholas leaves Loma Linda University Medical Center just 18 days after receiving his new heart. *Courtesy of Anthony R. Portillo, LLUMC Audio-Visual Services.*

Tom and Jayne with their son just minutes before the heart transplant surgery on April 26, 1986.

A playful boy only eight days after surgery. *Courtesy of Anthony R. Portillo, LLUMC Audio-Visual Services.*

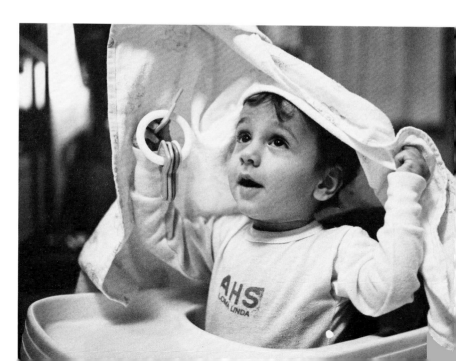

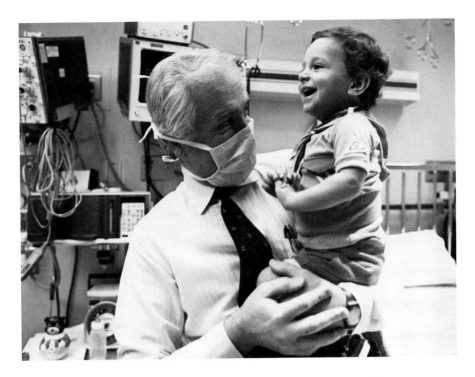

Dr. Leonard L. Bailey, the pediatric cardiac surgeon at Loma Linda University Medical Center says good-bye to Nicholas, christened "Baby James" for media purposes, only eighteen days after our son received his new heart. *Courtesy R. Portillo, LLUMC Audio-Visual Services.*

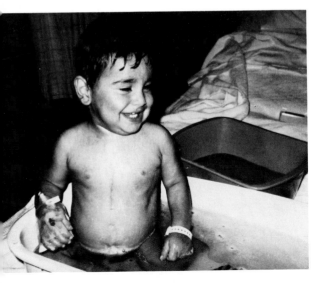

Bathtime in the hospital, June 22, 1986, while being treated for organ rejection. Only the pencil-thin incision extending along his breastbone remains as a tell-tale sign of his incredible ordeal.

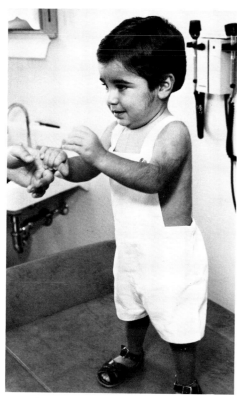

Two glimpses of Nicholas at the transplant patient clinic the Tuesday before he dies. *Courtesy Duane R. Miller, LLUMC Audio-Visual Services.*

Due to this lack of control, private adoptions were not "blessed" by the state with automatic MediCal coverage. It was neither equitable nor fair.

Diane warned us, however, that trying to get the state to do what was right would be a time-consuming process. She didn't guarantee success but felt that it was certainly worth trying. This was good news, because obviously Nicholas needed all the medical coverage he could get.

But we were distressed to learn that, because of the new red tape involved with these efforts, the processing of Nicholas' adoption papers wouldn't be final until his MediCal status had been decided once and for all. We had been anxiously preparing for the adoption to be official sometime in late August or early September. Now we had no idea when it would happen.

This made Tom more than a little nervous, because he knew that until the day the adoption was official in the eyes of the law, Nicholas' birthmother could have a change of heart and begin proceedings to have him returned to her—a legal contest that birthmothers typically win. But Jayne kept saying that she had a good feeling about the woman, that she had made an important, courageous, and determined decision for herself and Nicholas. Jayne believed instinctively—though we'd never met her—that the birthmother would abide by her part of the bargain.

Regardless, Tom's agitation grew as the process dragged on. He just wanted the whole matter to be over—to have his son *be in fact his son* without the nagging worry that something might go wrong. Hadn't we all been through enough already? While Tom worried himself into a knot, Jayne remained calm and sure.

Nicholas continued to be a cheerful, happy child who not only enjoyed playing with Mom, Dad, and Kipling; he also appeared content by himself. In the morning, right after waking, he'd typically lie in his crib, scrutinizing his hands or a toy—especially his colorful plastic keys. He also got a big kick out of talking to himself. One early sound experiment that lasted a month or so was coughing—not because he was ill, but for the joy of creating a new sound; then he'd giggle at his own inventiveness. Whether making up new sounds or meticulously studying a book or rattle, he usually was content for a half-hour to an hour before crying out.

Our baby was changing. In fact, he wasn't really a baby any more. He was developing a personality, becoming a *little boy,* becoming a real little person right before our eyes! It was marvelous to watch a body grow, a mind develop!

ᘒ

Early in September, Nicholas had his first visit with his new cardiologist. Recommended to us by Dr. Rubenstein, Dr. Auerbach dealt almost entirely with children with heart problems. With graying hair, a fondness for western string ties, and a cheerful demeanor, he decorated his office with drawings from his young patients and the many letters to the editor he'd had published in newspapers over the years.

On this visit he told us, "Nicholas is doing well. But I'm concerned that if he catches a cold, it could easily become pneumonia."

Though we'd always been diligent about not exposing Nicholas to people with illnesses, now we were on alert more than ever.

By the middle of September, Tom's outside freelancing and Jayne's work overlapped, so that Nicholas needed a babysitter for four hours a day on Wednesday and Friday. We asked Tom's mom and, with a little reassurance—after all, it had been twenty-seven years since she'd had a baby in the house—she agreed.

The first time Jayne dropped Nicholas off, she explained our policy of never calling Nicholas by any variation of that name. "Oh, I understand," said Grandma Alice. "Nich-O-las." Her pronunciation tended to stress the middle syllable in a very dear way. "I'll always call him Nich-O-las."

For his part, Nicholas wasn't particularly happy being left behind that afternoon, but he quickly learned that there was someone besides Mom and Dad who loved him dearly. Grandma

Alice became very comfortable with her little grandson, and he learned to enjoy the new and different stimulation. By the end of the second visit, they were great pals. After having brought up three boys, Grandma found that watching Nicholas was easier than she'd anticipated. She learned how to give him his medications, helped him practice drinking from a cup, and fashioned exercise games to strengthen his skinny legs. When Tom picked him up after work, it was obvious that Nicholas was perfectly happy.

About this time, we all learned a couple of tricks that were guaranteed to get a wide-grinned, sparkling-eyed chuckle out of Nicholas. For some reason, he found other people's sneezing and coughing *very* funny. And an exaggerated sneeze or cough was hilarious.

"Ah . . . ahhh . . . ahhhh . . . *ahhhh . . . choo-o-o-o!* Hack—hack! Ah . . . ahhh . . . ahhhh . . . *ahhhh . . . choo!*" It was pure joy to see Nicholas and his grandma laughing and giggling, sneezing and coughing.

Grandma Alice also lavished her grandson with new pajamas and brightly colored toys—from key rings (just in case Mom forgot to pack them in the diaper bag) to pop beads to musical maracas. His twice-weekly visits with Grandma Alice were looked forward to by all. Certainly Tom's mom appeared ten years younger overnight. Nicholas, on the other hand, was showing his age: by late September, he was creeping at such high speed that Grandma could only just keep up with him!

We found out, too, that the imp in Grandma was alive and well. One evening, Jayne stopped by to pick up our little guy. After a brief chat about how he'd been that day, Grandma stooped to hug her grandson. "Come to Grandma, Nicky." When she realized what she'd said, she quickly amended herself, ". . . er . . . Nich-O-las," pretending nothing had happened.

But the jig was up. And there wasn't a lot we could do. Grandmothers have rights, too. Though she tried to cover it up, we knew that to her, her grandson had become her little Nicky.

ᵕᵉ§

In October, when Nicholas was nine months old, we returned to Stanford for the annual Intensive Care Nursery graduates reunion. Nicholas was dressed in a blue-and-white sailor suit complete with gold braid piping, blue knee socks, and oxford shoes. The nurses were astounded. They recognized us, so this little boy in Tom's arms had to be Nicholas. We were bursting with pride to show off our son; he looked so healthy and normal! His eyes danced brightly as Mary—his one-time night nurse—presented him with his first-ever helium balloon. We tied it around his wrist, and he had a grand time bopping it around. (He played with that balloon for the entire next week.)

When Dr. Stevenson saw his former patient, his eyes took on a misty look. He turned to his young daughter, who was next to him, saying, "This little boy was one of the sickest children your daddy ever took care of." Then to us, "In all my years in neonatal medicine, I've seen hundreds of sick babies come and go. But I've never seen a baby as sick as Nicholas who survived." His straightforward statement served once again to underscore our tremendous pride in our son—of his survival, of his miracle, of his happy development, and of *our* accomplishment together as a family. We could only pray that it would continue.

As a band played and clowns delighted the crowd, the afternoon passed. We saw many of the doctors, nurses, and therapists who had been instrumental in helping us bring Nicholas home. We gave each a summary of Nicholas' progress and thanked them for the care they'd given him. At afternoon's end, the three of us were exhausted. It felt wonderful to be back home.

ᵕᵉ§

Tom's late-October birthday was coming up fast. As it neared he thought wistfully about treating himself to some time—enough to finish his book once and for all. Through this pleasant daydream, however, he saw that the facts were unassailable. Despite his time being more flexible since the layoff, he really had no choice but to put his writing on a back burner. The responsibilities and joys of fathering simply kept him scurrying, not to mention employment leads, job interviews, and countless hours at free-lance assignments. Then, the next thing he knew, three months of being at home with his family came to an end. He started a new full-time job a week before his birthday. Once again he was edit-ing computer-related publications.

And, just as we expected, the benefits coordinator was quick to point out that "preexisting conditions" within the family wouldn't be covered by the company's insurance carrier. Now more than ever, we slept easier knowing that Nicholas had CCS coverage and understood how important it was that our attorney be able to arrange for MediCal.

కాక

In early fall, Fr. Dempsey called us to say he required surgery on his right leg. One Saturday we piled into the car and drove up to St. Mary's Hospital in San Francisco to visit our lanky friend. When we showed up at his door, he was in bed and deeply in-volved in a phone conversation. He saw us, winked, grinned, and pointed to the solitary chair in the room.

"Look, that baby you're going to have—and you're going to have it, mind you!—is going to make some people very happy. . . . Yes, I understand your situation. . . . Look, I'm going to give you a number. The people there'll be able to help you. . . ." Ten minutes later he wrapped up the latest details in the life of a scared soul he'd taken under his wing.

"Jayne, Tom, and Nicholas—thank you for coming! I'm sorry, but I can't get out of bed without the help of one of these people in white coats. Let me show you something."

He threw back the sheets and revealed an eighteen-inch incision on his leg, closed with dozens of staple sutures. Despite this, he couldn't wait to get a close look at Nicholas. He took our son and held him high in the air. Nicholas looked a little concerned at first, then sat contentedly on Fr. Dempsey's good knee and listened to a story about how special it was to be loved and cared about. Our friend then described a national project he was working on with Archbishop O'Connor of New York to provide housing and clothing for unwed pregnant mothers.

Before we left, Tom made a point of reminding Fr. Dempsey that it was right after he baptized Nicholas that our son suddenly veered away from the edge of eternity. Fr. Dempsey waved the praise aside and reminded Tom that it was all in Hands greater than ours. We left, not knowing how close to eternity our special friend was himself. Though we talked again on the phone, this was our last visit. He died October 28, 1985.

On Halloween Nicholas came down with his first cold. We went on alert, but he handled it without complication, just like a normal little boy. We spent a quiet day by a toasty fire. In the late afternoon, Mommy dressed him in a clown suit from his Grandma Alice and painted his face with a little red heart on one cheek and a polka dot on the other. He thought this was all quite funny, and we got some great photos that day.

Jayne and Nicholas spent a lot of time indoors now, because the chilly days were upon us. Reading stories and playing with Mickey Mouse were favorite activities. Nicholas laughed and played with Mickey, held him up and jabbered away at him. He treated Mickey not like a doll or a teddy bear but like a real person. His face lit up each morning when he first spied Mickey in the corner of his crib; he'd grin from ear to ear. We were certain that our boy thought he had a brother. Jayne sometimes mimicked Mickey's voice as she held him in front of Nicholas, squeaking, "Hi, Nicholas. My name is Mickey Mouse." Nicholas would squint at Mickey, perplexed that his buddy could talk so well. Not surprisingly, a Mickey Mouse theme developed around Nicholas. There were Mickey pictures on his nursery wall, on his drinking cup, on his ball, and on his bath towel.

He developed quickly in the weeks between Thanksgiving and Christmas. He learned to hold a spoon and eat finger food, clap his hands, and—most exciting of all—pull himself up and stand, first in his crib, then anywhere he could get a handhold.

Around this time, Jayne taught him two new games that underscored how well he was developing. One was "Clap for Mommy." Some of our happiest moments came when we asked Nicholas to "Clap for Mommy" or "Clap for Daddy." He would bring the palms of his hands together—sometimes gently, sometimes with a smack, but always with a special gleam in his eye, a radiant smile on his face, and an air of vast accomplishment. The pride and love that filled us to overflowing at these times cannot be adequately described.

Another game was "Where's Nicholas?" One needed only to ask "Where's Nicholas?" and our son would cover his eyes with his little hands and peek through his fingers. It was simply a version of peekaboo, but the concentrated love and delight, the enchanted smiles, and the sparkling giggles we all shared when playing these games were boundless.

He also learned to open and close drawers and cupboards. He loved to study anything with a hinge action—especially doors, cupboards, and books. Fascinated by his intense study of these simple mechanisms, we theorized that he might become an engineer someday. Certainly *curious* and *busy* were the words that best described Nicholas at this stage.

One day he discovered the living room bookshelf. Because we love books, we wanted to encourage Nicholas' interest, so we were in a bit of a quandary regarding how to discipline him when he decided to become a one-man demolition squad. In minutes he'd have dozens of books scattered all over the floor, propping himself up with one hand in the middle of a pile, using the other to twist and rip pages and gloriously crack spines! It was clearly great fun. If he happened to lay himself down in the pile so that he had both hands free, he inspected the way a book functioned, how it was bound, how he could open and close it—but he tore it up in the process. The solution was to move Mommy and Daddy's books to shelves out of his reach and devote the lower shelves to Nicholas' books. At this point, though obviously he was too young to understand reading, we were so pleased that he took an interest in books that we let him do whatever he wanted with his own. It was only a matter of time before even the most sturdy children's book became a tattered remnant of its original self.

Now that Nicholas was "getting into things," it was more important than ever that we parented and disciplined consistently. We'd seen many instances of parents who didn't understand that they had to show a united front. To have one parent say, "Go to your room for twenty minutes," and the other five minutes later say, "It's okay to come out now," was asking for anarchy. To say, "If you do X, I'll punish you," and then watch X being done without following through, was abdicating authority in the child's eyes.

It became clear to us that if Nicholas couldn't trust us to follow through with clearly stated discipline, he couldn't trust *anything* we said or did. In the end, family unity, loyalty, and happiness were at stake—not just in the short run, but *for the duration of our family.*

We noted as well that Nicholas frequently "tested" us. Though he knew perfectly well that a particular living room lamp was off limits, we'd observe him "sneak up on it," then give us a sidelong glance, as though wondering, *Will the rule be enforced today?* Though 95 percent of the time it would be, he knew that sometimes Mommy and Daddy were oddly inconsistent. What he didn't know, and what we couldn't expect him to intuit, was that sometimes we were just too tired to say no. When we realized the potential for trouble inherent in this, we tried very hard, regardless of how exhausted we were, to be consistent in our discipline.

Still, as long as we both live, we'll never cease to treasure the memory of those elfin and surreptitious glances over his shoulder to check us out.

≈§

In the middle of November, Diane Michelson called to tell us that she'd been successful at getting Nicholas' MediCal petition approved. Nicholas now had dual health coverage. Even more important, this meant that his adoption paperwork could finally be processed. We had a court date in two and a half weeks!

December 4 arrived cold and crisp, though the sun was out and the skies were blue. We all awakened early. After all, this was a very important and special day. We dressed Nicholas in red-and-green plaid overalls over a baby tuxedo shirt with a red bow tie. His black-and-white oxfords completed the outfit. He looked mighty dapper for a nine-and-one-half-month-old boy!

We met Diane early at the county courthouse and were ushered into the judge's chambers. The atmosphere was very formal. The judge, who sat behind his desk in his black robes, opened a file and shuffled papers, glancing at some and reading others. Finally he looked up, smiled at us, and asked Diane if we were ready. His gaze lingered on Nicholas, who sat quietly on Tom's lap rubbing his fists in his eyes.

Then he asked, "Do you, Thomas and Jayne Miller, promise to love and take care of this child here present and all his needs until he reaches maturity?"

We responded solemnly, "We do."

"Will you freely grant him all the rights you would a biological child, including those of inheritance?"

"We will."

The judge then placed one hand firmly on the papers, looked directly at us, and his smile broadened. "Then I am pleased and proud to tell you that this young man today, now, and forevermore shall be known as Nicholas Lawrence Miller!"

With Jayne's hand tightly holding his arm, Tom glowed inside as he'd never done before. It was the happiest and proudest day of his entire life!

Chapter Eight

Christmas lay just around the corner, and Nicholas attained two more milestones—one big and one small. The lesser achievement: Nicholas got his first haircut. This was really a treat, since he'd come home from the hospital with his head completely shaved and his hair had taken its time growing back out.

Three days after the haircut, Jayne couldn't wait for Tom to come home from work to tell him of Nicholas' latest feat. "Darling," she said over the phone, "Nicholas crawled today. He *really* crawled . . . about six feet!" Tom couldn't wait to see for himself, but he rushed home in vain. It would be another two weeks before Nicholas felt confident enough about this new method of locomotion to try again.

On the Saturday before Christmas, we took Nicholas to a local mall to see Santa Claus. This particular Santa offered to videotape five minutes of your child sitting on his lap. Behind us in line was a lady holding a little boy about Nicholas' age. As we stood talking between ourselves, she spoke to us. "Is this your son?"

"Yes."

"Honestly, never in my life have I seen such a handsome little boy, and he's so *mature*-looking."

"Thank you, we're very proud of him." We turned away, our chests puffed out. Here was a woman apparently *with her very own adorable child in her arms* who was moved to compliment our child over her own.

What was it about Nicholas? Charisma was one thing. But where did it come from? What did it mean? Tom, always the proud father, loved to extrapolate: "I just *know* he's going to be a senator someday." But there was more to it. Because these compliments were almost always coupled with a reference to his looking mature, we wondered if his first nine weeks of struggling to live hadn't somehow imbued his spirit with *experience.* He looked mature because he had in fact gone through more in those short weeks than most people go through in a lifetime.

The next evening, we put up a half-height noble fir tree on the sideboard in the front window. In our family, Tom—who claimed still to be twelve years old inside, who was enchanted by movies, planetariums, and laser shows, *and* who once had come within a hair's breadth of starting a light-show business—was responsible for putting the lights on the tree, while Jayne always hung the many unique ornaments we'd collected over the years. On this particular evening, though, Jayne was at work, so Nicholas helped Daddy. The first thing to do was to unravel the lights and pull the cord out straight. Tom always did this by first plugging the lights into the wall. With the colored lights on, he could better see what he was doing. Nicholas took one look at the string of glowing colored lights and—well, it was obvious to Tom that his son was a chip off the old block.

But it was also obvious that the lights would never get hung if Nicholas' fascination wasn't controlled somewhat. So Nicholas got to play in his Johnny Jump-Up while Tom finished his half of the Christmas tree decorating. The next morning, Jayne decorated the tree and hung stockings and an evergreen garland on the stone hearth before assembling our Christmas teddy bear collection on the mantle.

Christmas morning arrived. The choir at our church sang all the seasonal favorites so well that the congregation was moved to applaud. Nicholas was taken aback by this. He looked to his left. He looked to his right. He looked over our shoulders. People were clapping throughout the church. We could almost read his thoughts: *Hey, that's my trick!* Then, when the applause had stopped, Nicholas began clapping. *Now, that's better!*

After church we gathered with our families, and Nicholas was inundated with presents from grandparents, great-grandmothers, and relatives *ad infinitum.* Wearing a white sweatshirt that announced in brilliant green, red, and yellow letters, "MY FIRST CHRISTMAS ON EARTH," he ripped the brilliant wrapping off a blue-and-yellow plastic kiddie car with a horn that actually beeped. But it was the paper-shredding that interested him, not the present. He was a little young yet to appreciate his good fortune. When he was through tearing and scrunching the first wrapping, he began exploring another package that was set before him. He inspected it tentatively at first; then, when his careful examination was completed, he tore into it with gusto—and found a red-and-white spotted horse that made clip-clop sounds as it rolled along. When we pushed him along on either of these treasures, he squealed happily.

Then Christmas was over, New Year's Day 1986 came and went, and our California air grew chill. During those weeks, Nicholas learned to stand up behind his car and horse and push them across the room as he cautiously took his first unaccompanied steps.

Despite these extremely tentative walking experiments, he'd clearly decided that crawling was far more efficient than either rolling or creeping. Within a few weeks of his first attempt at crawling, that child *knew* the world was his to conquer! And we, in our turn, responded by child-proofing like crazy.

Sometimes Nicholas took an inevitable tumble or pinched his exploring fingers in a drawer. At such times, we tried very hard not to overreact. Usually we'd be right by his side to help out and offer a kiss or word of sympathy; but then we'd always remind him, "It's all part of growing up, Nicholas." We didn't want to program him into becoming a crying little manipulator, as some parents unconsciously do when they shower each and every one of childhood's little scrapes with everything from tears to sweets.

Yet there was bad to go with the good. By late January, Jayne and Nicholas both had weathered three colds. No sooner did one start feeling well than the other came down with something. Although Jayne at one point developed pneumonia, Nicholas kept bouncing back from his colds just fine. Dr. Auerbach was sufficiently impressed that Nicholas did so well—not only with the colds but just generally—that he decided it was time to try changing Nicholas' quinidine schedule to every eight hours. Just to be on the safe side, he ordered another twenty-four-hour portable heart monitor study to be done at home. The study looked normal, and we were all encouraged.

꿎

We were outgrowing the space in our tiny country house. After considerable thought and financial review, we decided to look for a new home. We agreed that, after we were settled into a new home, it would be time to begin another adoption search so that Nicholas could have a brother or a sister. We began 1986, then, with our goals for that year firmly established!

On the last day of January, Nicholas sat up straight without having to hold himself upright with one arm. We were thrilled! Developmentally, he was moving right along, and now both his hands were free. If we thought he was a one-man demolition squad before . . . *look out!*

In February it rained. We built roaring fires and had lots of indoor playtime. Jayne busily planned Nicholas' first birthday party. We wanted to have a special christening ceremony that same day. He'd been baptized, of course, but we had missed sharing the experience with family, friends, and the church community; in addition, we wanted to share the miracle of Nicholas' first year and speak our thanks to the many who had participated with, encouraged, and supported us and our little boy.

Despite torrents of rain and a howling wind, we all gathered inside our church. Fr. Miles invited all those gathered to personally draw a cross on Nicholas' forehead to welcome our son into the Christian community. We sang one of Nicholas' favorite songs: "It's a brand new day, everything is fine; though it may be gray, I want you to know that the sun's gonna shine. . . ." Nicholas, who was dressed in a white sailor suit with short pants, looked all around as if to say, "I know that song; I hear it often at home. How is it that all these people know my song?"

Before the actual baptism began, Fr. Miles reached into the

pocket of his vestments and brought out a little vial. He held it in the air and explained, "Recently I visited the Holy Land. While I was there—well, this is water from the River Jordan."

He opened the vial and poured the water over Nicholas' forehead, proclaiming the words, "I baptize you in the name of the Father, and of the Son, and of the Holy Spirit."

We then opened up the church hall for a birthday party. Balloons, hats, cake, and cups were all decorated with—of course!—Mickey Mouse. The guest of honor, who had spent the first half of the baptism ceremony quiet and very serious but had squirmed in his father's arms during the second half, promptly fell asleep as his many fans celebrated. Many of the people who'd watched him at Stanford and cared about him through his illness also gathered with us that day.

We awakened the birthday boy for his cake and to have him say goodbye to his guests. He wasn't very happy about being disturbed, but when Jayne's father wrapped a bouquet of helium balloons around his wrist and began to help his grandson learn the fine art of jumping, Nicholas perked up as though to say, "Now this is more like it!" We were very proud of him. And all too soon the party ended.

That night Nicholas kissed Mommy on the cheek for the first time. This of course elicited quite a positive reaction, so by the next day he would pucker up his lips whenever he wanted to give us kisses. To love a child is a wonderful experience; to experience him learning to love back is indescribable.

In early March, we had a spell of absolutely beautiful weather. The rains were replaced by crisp blue cloudless skies and bright sunshine. The magnolia tree in front was blooming, and our spring bulbs were emerging: over a hundred tulips—yellow, deep purple, bright scarlet, lavender, and some that were rippled with two and three colors. There were also daffodils, both yellow and white, irises, crocuses, and a multitude of other flowers. Soon the Miller garden was an Easter basket of color.

Nicholas' changing table overlooked this gorgeous array, and sometimes, as Jayne tended to her little boy and her eyes fell on the profusion below, she remembered wistfully back to a year before, to the morning when we had raced to see Nicholas for the first time. That day she had glimpsed our first daffodil blooming, an early bloom. The second wouldn't open for three more weeks, on the morning after Nicholas rallied—the morning after Fr. Dempsey had magically appeared over our son.

We also visited Central Park often to let Nicholas swing in the baby swings. He laughed and laughed and pumped his legs as if he knew instinctively that this would make him go faster and higher. He was quite the adventurer and even threw his arms in the air as he yelped with pure happiness at the rapid swinging motion. Never could joy be more concentrated.

We watched and quietly marveled that this little boy had, only twelve months before, lain critically ill in a hospital intensive care ward. Clearly our son had learned to love life and experience it fully.

Our thoughts that Easter season were filled with memories of those first nine weeks of Nicholas' life. As themes of rebirth and resurrection abounded, we couldn't help but remember our own Lenten-like experience. As Jesus had spent forty days of penitence in the desert, we too had searched our souls in Stanford's East Nursery and, in our trial, opened ourselves to the raw power of God. The number of our days had been sixty-three. From each desert came renewal and strengthened faith.

Our home was now up for sale, and during most of March we toured prospective buyers around the property. Nicholas simply enjoyed people; the more the merrier. He drank up all the attention he was getting from the steady stream of visitors, greeting each one with a grin and apparently basking in their many compliments.

We spent hours in our garden that spring, tending to the flowers, weeding, and keeping the lawns trimmed so that the house would show well. Nicholas absolutely loved crawling around the lawns and would grab great clumps of grass in eager delight, then look around to make sure we'd appreciated his accomplishment.

In mid March, we went away on our first overnight trip since Nicholas' birth. Katie and her husband took care of our son while we visited the Monterey Bay Aquarium, shopped in Carmel, and walked along the beach. We even enjoyed a romantic dinner and went to a late movie. After thirty-six hours away, we were refreshed yet eager to get back to our little boy. Nicholas, in the meantime, had found a grand playmate in Auntie Katie. He cried only twice—when we left and when he saw us walk back in the door!

Our home sold quickly, and on Easter Sunday—following a tearful service wherein we celebrated not only Christ's resurrection but our own miracle boy—we rushed to put a deposit on a much larger soon-to-be-built house in the East Bay. We were excited at the prospect of moving in late June.

⋘

Tuesday, April first. Nicholas awakened with yet another cold. His nose was runny and he had a slight temperature. Because he was teething, he chewed on anything he could put in his mouth and was generally fussy. Later that day his temperature went up to 104. The physician taking calls for Dr. Rubenstein ordered Nicholas on antibiotics. By Friday, although his temperature had returned to normal, Nicholas looked pale and his breathing was rapid. He had little appetite and coughed often.

We awakened early on Saturday morning. It was dark out, and the clock read 5:50 A.M. Nicholas just plain didn't feel well.

And he refused his morning bottle.

This was totally unprecedented! Clearly something was wrong. Our call to Dr. Rubenstein went right through to her, and she said she'd meet us at District Hospital in thirty minutes.

The chest X-ray told the story. Nicholas had pneumonia in his right lung and showed signs of early congestive heart failure. Dr. Rubenstein arranged to have Nicholas admitted to the hospital and started him on antibiotics and oxygen.

Nicholas wasn't happy. He obviously felt terrible, found himself thrust into a new environment, and objected to being forced to wear oxygen tubing in his nose. Once he'd settled down and accepted the inevitable, however, he slept much of the day. He took fluids better by that evening but had no appetite for solid food. We made plans to alternate spending the night in his room, as we had during his last hospitalization. One of us was always to be with him.

On Sunday Dr. Auerbach came to examine Nicholas, then spoke at great length with Tom. Jayne was at home napping. When she arrived back at the hospital, she found Nicholas asleep in Tom's arms. She sensed immediately that Tom was very worried. When she asked him if he was concerned about something, he nodded but put his finger to his lips and pointed to his sleeping son. Jayne's stomach ached. She felt anxious and afraid. Without being told, she knew that bad news was about to be shared. Her thoughts raced: *Now hang on to yourself, Jayne,* she said to herself. *Until a few days ago, Nicholas was progressing beautifully. Only two and a half weeks ago we saw the cardiologist and he gave Nicholas a glowing report.* Despite the silent pep talk, however, she knew something was very wrong.

Nicholas awoke suddenly and held out his arms for Mommy. She cuddled her son—still pale and with mussed hair, the oxygen tubing still in his nose—and crooned her own version of his favorite song.

> Silent night, holy night!
> Son of God, love's pure light
> Radiant beams from thy holy face,
> With the dawn of redeeming grace . . .
> *Sleep in heavenly peace,*
> *Sleep in heavenly peace.*

Nicholas always responded to this carol—originally written as a lullaby; it never failed to calm him. Even this time, he fell right back to sleep. Tom sat pensively in a rocking chair, watching his wife and son. Nicholas awoke again later and was less fussy. We read stories, sang songs, and clapped hands. Jayne's parents came to visit just as Nicholas' dinner tray was delivered. He took a few bites from Grandpa, who provided airplane noises to accompany each spoonful. He tired of the game quickly, however, and refused any further food. While Grandma and Grandpa were there, Jayne and Tom stepped out for a few minutes so that she could find out what was worrying Tom.

"Darling," he began, "Dr. Auerbach came to see Nicholas today, and we had a long talk. He feels that it's very likely that there's nothing more he can do to help Nicholas. He's concerned that Nicholas got so sick so fast and feels it's probable this will happen often in the future. He needs to run more tests, but basically he feels that the only thing medical science may be able to offer Nicholas now is a heart transplant."

Tom's eyes filled with tears and Jayne, now pale, fell into Tom's arms. "Somehow we'll handle it, Tommy, but right now I feel terribly scared and sad. Our little guy has already been through so much. Somehow this just doesn't seem fair."

Holding hands tightly, we walked back to Nicholas' room. Jayne's parents were ready to leave, and she walked out with them to say goodbye and tell them the news she herself had just heard.

During the next several days, Nicholas improved steadily, and Thursday we left the hospital with instructions to go to the University of California Medical Center in San Francisco on Monday for an extensive echocardiogram, and then to see Dr. Auerbach in his office on Tuesday.

Katie agreed to accompany Jayne and Nicholas to San Francisco for the test. The day was bright and sunny, and Nicholas looked all around at the new sights and played with the steering wheel on his stroller as Jayne pushed him up the hill to the hospital. They entered an examination room filled with a large screen and extensive computerized equipment. The pleasant technician asked some preliminary questions about Nicholas' history, while Nicholas, an old hand at examinations by this time, sat on the exam table intently looking around as Jayne held his hand.

"We'll be giving Nicholas medication to put him to sleep," the technician said.

"I don't understand," Jayne objected immediately. "Nicholas has had several echoes at Stanford and has always been very cooperative and well behaved."

The technician countered, "Yes, Mrs. Miller, but he wasn't fourteen months old back then."

"Nevertheless," Jayne quietly but firmly replied, "I'd like you at least to attempt the test without any sedation. Otherwise I simply won't sign the consent." He stepped out to check with the physician in charge.

Jayne remarked to Katie, "You know, this is classic. How often do patients receive treatment or medication simply because it's the 'proper' protocol or routine? What if Nicholas is allergic to chloral hydrate?"

The doctor reluctantly agreed to let the test begin without sedation. Should Nicholas become restless, however, the medication would be given without further discussion. Nicholas settled down on the exam table for the study and smiled and giggled his way through it. The entire procedure took nearly an hour and, when it was completed, the technician pronounced Nicholas "a magnificent child." Jayne beamed and said thank you, and Katie winked at Jayne and gave Nicholas a big hug.

At Dr. Auerbach's office the next day, he said that the echo results only confirmed his belief that a heart transplant was necessary. Because of her work, Jayne knew that the philosophy of when to perform transplants had changed over the years. In the early days, a patient had to be literally moments from death for the experimental surgery to be performed. Now, however, it was generally agreed that the healthier the patient was at the time of transplant, the better the chances for a successful outcome.

In Nicholas' case, his heart was severely damaged, but his other organs were healthy; his chances for survival and a return to normal life were therefore good. And because we'd done so well with Nicholas' medication schedule thus far, he doubted we'd have difficulty with post-transplant home treatment. He'd already spoken to the MediCal/CCS office, which agreed with his assessment of Nicholas as a transplant candidate and ourselves as a "compliant family."

"However," he went on, "the only heart transplant facility in California that CCS/MediCal will qualify for payment is Stanford. And because I'm not on staff there, I won't be able to follow Nicholas any longer; one of their cardiologists will be taking over."

"We understand," Jayne said, feeling drained, aware of a creeping numbness throughout her being. "But is Stanford truly the only option?"

"Yes. As far as MediCal is concerned, they have the most experience."

Though we'd known for several days that Nicholas was likely to need a transplant, the reality that our lives were about to change irrevocably and dramatically began to settle in. Since the family's ability to comply with an involved post-transplant home-care program was critical for acceptance, we needed to prepare for a more intensive commitment than we had yet known—perhaps even a major reordering of our lives. To what extent, we were yet to learn.

As Nicholas played happily on the floor between us that evening, we wept uncontrollably. It just didn't seem fair. For one entire year he had done so well. He looked so good, and he had developed into such a handsome, happy, good-natured little boy who obviously loved life. He thrived on love and normalcy.

How could we possibly be asked to play God with his precious life?

WHY?

Chapter Nine

Though only a few days earlier, Nicholas had lain pale and lethargic in a hospital crib, he quickly bounced back. His cheeks glowed with rosy fire, and his eyes sparkled with the curiosity of toddlerhood. For hours each day, he pulled his books off the shelf (dozens of times), explored the contents of his toy box, and practiced walking while holding onto Mommy's index finger. He was just fourteen months old.

He'd been home with us exactly one year.

Jayne awoke early on April 16. Tom and Nicholas still slept, and our tiny house seemed especially dark and quiet. Thoughts whirled; they centered around "the transplant." *This will be like waiting to find a baby to adopt. I wonder how long it will be until they find a compatible heart. Since Nicholas looks so healthy, will they accept him right away, or will he be put on a low-priority list until he becomes more severely symptomatic?*

The darkness intensified her uneasiness. Her thoughts turned to prayer. *Please, Lord, bless and guide Tom and me as we seek the best care for Nicholas. Give us courage to face yet another medical crisis. Continue to bless Nicholas with his wonderfully happy disposition. Teach us patience as we wait for a heart to be donated. And especially give courage to the parents of an innocent young life who'll be asked to donate their child's heart so that our little boy may live.*

Calmed, she allowed her thoughts to drift again and decided that nothing needed to be done for a few weeks; she could put off calling Stanford for the time being. She dozed off until the alarm clock jarred the house awake at seven.

As she slipped on her robe, she remembered her earlier train of thought, and her resolve to wait weeks disappeared. She announced to Tom, "I'm going to call Loma Linda Medical Center today to see if they have any grant money available for Nicholas.

Because they've done the most infant human heart transplants, I have to hear what they have to say. I'm not comfortable with Stanford's being our only option. They've never done a transplant on an infant."

Tom finished shaving and said, "Sounds like a good plan. Gather as much information as you possibly can, darling, and we'll discuss our options tonight."

Nicholas mugged and chirped his way through breakfast. Never a big eater, he enjoyed graham crackers and bananas that morning. While her son ate, Jayne sat at the kitchen table and began preparing a file folder and a list of questions to ask the transplant coordinators at both Stanford and Loma Linda. The morning passed quickly, with bathtime and playtime. Then, while Nicholas napped, Jayne began making calls.

"Loma Linda University Medical Center," the PBX operator answered clearly.

"I'd like to speak to the infant heart transplant coordinator, please."

"That would be Cheri Mathis," came the cheerful reply. "I'll put you through to her extension right away."

A moment later, Jayne heard a happy, almost girlish voice say, "Cheri Mathis."

"Hello, Cheri. This is Jayne Miller calling from northern California. Our fourteen-month-old son has been referred for a heart transplant." Jayne went on to explain Nicholas' history and gave her the results of his most recent echocardiogram. She also shared with Cheri our dilemma: that CCS/MediCal gave us only one transplant option, Stanford.

"As responsible parents, we're concerned. Stanford has done only one young child, and she was two years old. We know of Dr. Leonard Bailey's work through press coverage of Baby Fae. And later, when he helped Baby Moses and Baby Eve—the first two human-to-human infant heart transplant recipients—we learned still more about him. Would he possibly consider examining Nicholas?"

Cheri responded warmly, "Our administration will work closely with you. Please don't be worried about the financial aspect; costs are the least important factor right now. Restoring Nicholas' health should be everyone's primary concern. I'll speak to Dr. Bailey about Nicholas and get back to you tomorrow morning. Before we hang up, though, I want to talk with you briefly about our program."

Jayne continued jotting notes as she listened. "Nicholas may wait weeks, probably several months, for a heart—possibly even years. We require a nine-month relocation to the Loma Linda area, because follow-up care requires frequent hospital visits, tests, and medication adjustments."

Jayne gulped. "Nine months! Nine months is a very long time, Cheri. We have jobs to protect, careers to think about, and financial obligations. Is there any chance that follow-up care could be done closer to home, with perhaps monthly visits to Loma Linda? We have two transplant facilities relatively close to our home. Maybe Dr. Bailey knows someone on the staff at either Stanford or Pacific Presbyterian Medical Center he'd consider working with."

Cheri assured Jayne that she'd check with Dr. Bailey for his feedback on this. She empathized with the difficulties of turning our lives inside out.

"Oh, by the way, Jayne, do you know Nicholas' blood type?"

"I'll have to check on that," Jayne said. "I'll have that information for you tomorrow."

As she hung up, Jayne felt hopeful. It appeared that Nicholas would have at least two options open to him. She recopied her scribbled notes and organized them into her file. Then, noticing that the time had flown by, she rushed around getting ready for work. Soon Nicholas and she were on their way to Grandma Alice's house.

Indeed, Cheri did phone the next morning. "Hi, Jayne," she began. "Dr. Bailey believes it's important for Nicholas to be examined at Loma Linda. An appointment with the chief of pediatric cardiology will be necessary, as well as some preliminary tests. Can you arrange to have all of Nicholas' records forwarded as soon as possible?"

"Of course," Jayne said, and they scheduled tentative appointments for May 5 and 6.

Cheri went on: "While you're here, you and your husband will meet our social worker for a psychosocial evaluation."

"I see," said Jayne. "In other words, this whole presurgical workup will determine if Nicholas, as the patient, and we, as the family, are even eligible."

"That's right. But from everything I've learned, I wouldn't be concerned. You can also spend some time investigating housing possibilities around Loma Linda."

They were just wrapping up when Jayne remembered to give Cheri Nicholas' blood type.

"Okay, I've made a note of it," Cheri said. "We'll chat again soon. I'm looking into CCS/MediCal coverage for Nicholas at this end. Why don't you call your local representatives and check with them about whether they might reconsider Nicholas' case?"

Jayne next called Sue at the CCS office for our county. Though Sue was sympathetic to our search for experienced care for our son, she reiterated their policy: CCS/MediCal could approve only Stanford.

"You know, Mrs. Miller, Stanford has a fine reputation and has been a pioneering facility in heart transplantation."

"I'm aware of that, Sue, and I know that their success rate is wonderful for adults. But Nicholas is a baby, and as a caring parent I must seek the most experienced surgeon for heart transplants on babies."

Sue agreed to check with her MediCal director about whether they would approve Nicholas to have a medical workup at Loma Linda.

"I doubt that it can be done, but I'll give it a try."

A few hours later, she phoned back to say that, as she'd suspected, CCS/MediCal could authorize only Stanford for the preoperative evaluation as well as for the surgery.

Jayne managed to remain calm, though her anger at the system was building up inside. "Sue, to whom may I write to identify my problem and ask for an exception to be made?"

Sue rattled off a list of names and addresses of state-level directors of CCS and MediCal. "I wish you good luck and much success, Mrs. Miller. I must caution you, though, not to become too hopeful."

That night, after Nicholas had been sung to sleep and tucked in, we began drafting a letter stating our case.

Dear Doctor,

Imagine the dilemma we face as we are told that our fourteen-month-old son is in need of a heart transplant . . . only to be told that the only approved facility has never performed this procedure on anyone as young as our son. . . .

We ask that you consider granting approval to Dr. Leonard Bailey and Loma Linda University Medical Center. Surely you are aware of his recent successful infant transplant surgeries. . . .

About this time, the *San Francisco Catholic* monthly magazine ran a story about a young priest, Fr. Richard Bain, who celebrated healing Masses at St. Kevin's Church in San Francisco. According to the article, Fr. Bain claimed a high rate of success and had developed quite a following. Ordinarily we would have looked askance at such claims, but at this time in our lives, despite all the pain and frustration, our knowledge of God's presence and His guiding hand was as strong as ever. Nicholas had already been at the receiving end of one true miracle; who were we to judge another's claims of being a conduit of God's grace?

Jayne mentioned the article to her mother, who directed religious education for a South Bay parish. Her mom strongly encouraged us in opening our minds and hearts and giving Fr. Bain a chance.

The afternoon of April 21, we took Nicholas into San Francisco to St. Kevin's. The service began typically and progressed through the homily and communion. Then Fr. Bain, tall and in his midthirties (much younger than we'd anticipated), said to the congregation, "Those of you desiring God's healing power, please approach the altar by pews. But first, if there are any children to be healed, their parents may bring them up now."

We stood, and with Jayne holding Nicholas, who chose this moment to get fussy, we walked down the aisle to the altar. An assistant quickly arranged the dozen or so celebrants in a semicircle. When Fr. Bain approached us, he looked down at Nicholas and said, "Surely there's nothing wrong with this little boy. He looks so healthy."

"He's been recommended for a heart transplant, Father," Jayne said.

Fr. Bain's eyes opened wide; then he placed his large hand over Nicholas' chest and prayed: "May the heart beating in this little chest be renewed and transformed, and may the Lord provide you with all His healing strength and presence."

Nicholas calmed right down, and Fr. Bain moved on. Back at our seats, Nicholas smiled, ate vanilla wafers, and clapped his hands to the music during the remainder of the service as others waited peacefully at the altar, hoping to be touched by God.

Because we weren't expecting lightning to strike, we could do nothing but adopt an open-minded wait-and-see attitude and carry on with life.

The following week kept Jayne and Nicholas busy. They visited Jayne's maternal grandmother one afternoon, and Nicholas spoke his first "word." As he played on the floor while they chatted, he suddenly spied the bookshelf across the room. He crawled quickly over to it, pulled himself up to a standing position, touched the books, looked at Mommy and said, "Ba-ba-ba," then sqealed with delight. *Ba-ba-ba* became his operative word for books!

On Thursday Nicholas played with his second cousin Mark in the afternoon. Since both were first children, Mark and Nicholas lacked playmates, and Mark's mom, Maureen (who is Jayne's cousin), and Jayne decided to begin regular playtime get-togethers for their boys. Jayne had brought Mickey Mouse along, but Nicholas quickly put him aside as he began to play in Mark's Tupperware drawer.

The hour and a half they played was punctuated with quiet moments when they simply observed each other, as though asking themselves, *Who is this other little person? Since our eyes are at the same level, he has to be special . . . I think.*

As Jayne packed Nicholas' toys, she and Maureen made plans for Thursdays to become "playday." They agreed to be especially aware of any symptoms of illness so that neither child would be unnecessarily exposed.

Friday dawned clear and crisp. By midday, the air warmed and the bees hummed in the magnolia tree. Jayne and Nicholas watered the garden, and Nicholas played in the grass and freshly turned soil. He loved taking baths—particularly the splashing part—so he delighted in being given not one but two that day!

Later, dressed in a blue cotton-cord sailor suit with a zipper up the front, Nicholas discovered how to unzip the zipper. He soon learned that unzipping it meant that Mommy would zip it back up. He spent the afternoon testing this theory and yelped at her if he unzipped his suit and she didn't notice! Jayne had to work that day, so by one-thirty she and Nicholas were packed up and driving off to Grandma Alice's. It was April 25th.

A few minutes after three that afternoon, Jayne was involved in calibrating a complicated piece of equipment in the ICU at District Hospital. The patient census was high, and it would be a busy Friday night. One of Jayne's co-workers came over to give her a message.

"Cheri Mathis just phoned from Loma Linda. She wanted to talk to you, but I lost the connection as I tried to transfer the call. I think you'd better come over to the department and wait for her to call back. She seemed really anxious to talk to you."

"George, I simply don't have time to speak with her right now. Please tell her I'll return her call on Monday. I'm sure she wants to chat about our appointment ten days from now."

"Okay."

Moments later George returned, breathless. "Jayne, Cheri Mathis is on the phone again, and says she *must* speak to you right away."

Jayne strode briskly from the ICU to the Pulmonary Therapy Department, wondering what could be so urgent. *I don't even remember giving Cheri my work number,* she thought as she picked up the phone.

"Hi, Cheri, this is Jayne. How can I help you?"

"I have Dr. Bailey here to speak with you. He has a heart for Nicholas."

Chapter Ten

Jayne's own heart began to race. She heard it pounding in her ears. Her face felt warm and her knees weak. She slumped over a nearby counter, clutching the receiver to her right ear. Then she heard Dr. Bailey's quiet and caring voice.

"Mrs. Miller, I've received word of a heart available for transplant. The donor is an eighteen-month-old with the same blood type as your son. A cardiologist has examined the child and tested the heart. It's a good heart, and though I know this all seems sudden, I felt I had to call and discuss it with you. The history we have on Nicholas, his heart size, and recent bout of congestive failure and pneumonia all underscore his need for cardiac transplantation. We have other children waiting who are too small for this heart; I didn't want to turn this organ donation down without contacting you. I'm sure you have many questions, and I'll be glad to answer them."

Jayne's thoughts whirled. Tears welled in her eyes as a reply formed itself in her mind: *This is much too soon. Nicholas looks so healthy, and he's having a great time at his grandmother's house. Thank you so much for thinking of us, Doctor, but I don't think we're interested right now.*

Still she said nothing as a riot of thoughts and impressions raced in her mind. She felt mind-numbing fear. And hope. And confusion. And anger. *This is too soon!* Her knees grew even weaker. An image sprang up, uninvited, of our son on a cold operating table with his chest open and an anonymous green-clad surgeon standing over him, scalpel in hand. *No! No! It's not fair! Oh, God, why now? Why does this have to happen now? I don't want Nicholas' heart removed now. Not his heart!* Jayne shook her head hard to clear her thoughts. *God? God? Why are you doing this now?*

But this jumble of thoughts stayed locked in her mind as she strove to remain coherent on the phone with this soft-spoken, internationally renowned physician. "Dr. Bailey, I have several concerns that I need to discuss with you. But before any real decision can be made, I have to phone my husband for his input. And you should know that Cheri and I have discussed the financial situation. Nicholas is on MediCal and CCS, and they've told us repeatedly that they'll cover his transplant costs only if the operation is done at Stanford."

"Mrs. Miller," came the kind reply, "I can only tell you that our administration has sponsored the two earlier infant human transplants that were performed here, and they'll do the same for Nicholas. Please don't let finances alter your decision. Our primary concern is your son's complete recovery."

"Another topic I've discussed with Cheri," Jayne continued, "is your relocation policy of nine months. This would be impossible. Will you consider allowing us to return home within two or three months of the surgery? His follow-up needs could be taken care of at one of our local transplant facilities. And we'd gladly return to Loma Linda monthly for checkups."

"I think there's a strong possibility that we could manage that, given the proximity of Stanford and Pacific Presbyterian. I'm sure that something could be arranged with physicians there."

Having voiced these two concerns, Jayne then asked how soon the surgery would take place.

"I'd like you to speak to your husband as soon as possible, then fly down on the earliest available plane. If you decide to go ahead, we'd probably operate in the early morning. Nicholas would need some tests and medications as soon as you arrive."

Jayne hung up, paused to catch her breath, then called Tom at his office. Though she had been crying only moments before, she maintained her composure when he answered. She said, "Hi, darling. I have some big news to share. Are you sitting down?"

"Yes . . ."

"Tommy, Dr. Bailey from Loma Linda just called. They have a heart for Nicholas."

"Oh, no," he groaned. "Not now! This is the *worst* time. I've been so afraid it would happen this way. Ever since Dr. Auerbach told us, I've thought, *Okay, now what's the worst thing that could possibly happen?* The answer is always that Nicholas would be looking perfectly healthy, happy as a clam, our family content in every way—and then the call would come through that a heart was available. I couldn't imagine anything more devastating. Listen, Jayne, we can't make this decision by ourselves. We need the input of people who know what they're talking about. Call Dr. Rubenstein and Dr. Auerbach; ask their opinions. Then call me back."

For a moment, Tom sat numbly at his desk. He felt as if he'd been hit with a brick. Suddenly the stack of computer manuscripts on his desk were meaningless. He couldn't just *sit* there! He got up and began to pace—and think.

As with Jayne, an unwanted image sprang to mind: a scene from Mexican history—an Aztec priest poised over his semidivine sacrificial victim, razor-sharp obsidian knife in hand, beginning its long downward arc. . . .

He closed his eyes tightly and clenched his teeth to dispel the picture. He paced the aisle between cubicles, staying within earshot of his phone. *In these next minutes, we'd be making the most anguish-filled and important decision of our lives.*

Yet was there even a choice?

Despite Nicholas' healthy appearance, all indications underscored the prognosis that Nicholas would get progressively sicker. It was hard to believe, but it was only a matter of time until we would lose him.

Meanwhile, Jayne called Dr. Rubenstein. Laurie's immediate reply was, "You *have* to go for it!" Jayne, crying again, said, "Laurie, I'm so scared. I'm not ready to lose this little boy."

"I'll call Dr. Auerbach to get his advice and call you right back," Laurie offered.

In the meantime, Jayne explained the situation to her department director and then called airlines about available flights. She secured reservations for a nine o'clock flight.

As Jayne replaced the receiver, Laurie called back. "Dr. Auerbach and I agree that you should go for it. Dr. Bailey had spoken to him already, so he knew all about it. He and I both feel that this is a wonderful opportunity for Nicholas. Why don't you all just fly down and at least meet with Dr. Bailey? It will be easier to make a comfortable decision face to face. You can always opt not to go through with it if you don't like what you hear. It's just too important a decision to make from five hundred miles away."

Jayne agreed that this approach made good sense. She called Tom back and updated him, and we agreed to fly down to Loma Linda that evening.

Tom put the phone down and sought out his supervisor, saying, "I have something urgent to speak to you about. Let's find an empty conference room." Tom explained the dramatic turn in our lives and the need to drop all his work. In minutes, having secured a two-month leave of absence, Tom raced to his car.

Jayne called Dr. Bailey back, told him of our flight plans, and asked him whether Nicholas should be allowed any food or drink from this point on. He answered no.

Then he asked, "What name would you like Nicholas to be known as in the press? It's a good idea to use a press name to protect your privacy. Some have used wholly new names; Baby Fae's parents chose to use her middle name."

This caught Jayne off guard. She hadn't thought in terms of the press at all. Then she realized that she wouldn't have known about the earlier transplants, and wouldn't have contacted Loma Linda, if she hadn't become aware of them through the media. For a moment, she felt bewildered. She couldn't imagine Nicholas having any name other than his own. She thought of his middle name, Lawrence. *Baby Lawrence,* she mused. Suddenly she thought of Fr. Dempsey. *Fr. James Dempsey.* As a tribute to our incredible priest friend, she said to Dr. Bailey, "James. Use James as Nicholas' press name."

"Fine. Mrs. Miller, I'm looking forward to meeting you and your husband and Baby James as soon as you arrive. Have a safe flight to southern California."

In a state of semishock, but galvanized by the need for swift action, Jayne called Grandma Alice. "Mom, guess what? I've unexpectedly gotten a day off." The ruse was necessary; otherwise Tom's mom would worry herself sick. "Tom will be taking us all out to dinner, so please don't feed Nicholas, okay?"

"Okay, Jayne, we'll be all ready when you get here."

Assured that Nicholas wouldn't be eating, per Dr. Bailey's orders, Jayne now phoned her own parents to alert them to the trip we were about to take and the surgery Nicholas would probably be having in the next twelve hours. Her dad answered the telephone, having just arrived home from work.

"Dad, we're flying down to Loma Linda tonight. They have a heart for Nicholas." She began to cry.

"Honey, that's just the best news! This is exactly what we've all been hoping and praying for."

With her mind filled with fear at the *real* possibility of losing Nicholas, Jayne couldn't believe she had heard her dad right. Good news? Surely that wasn't the appropriate response. *They're going to remove Nicholas' heart from his body tomorrow!* Then she realized that her dad was trying his best to offer encouragement.

"I just know it will all work out," he was saying. "That little guy is just too special for anything to go wrong."

"I'm terribly scared, Dad. I don't want to lose my little boy. He's so perfect."

"Buck up, kiddo, and be brave. I'll tell Mom as soon as she gets home. We'll be praying. God bless you, honey."

Finally, she called her best friend. Katie, too, had just walked through the door, from a week away. She sounded out of breath as she picked up the phone.

"Katie, it's Jayne. You're not going to believe it, but Tom and Nicholas and I are flying to Loma Linda tonight. They have a heart for Nicholas."

"Oh, Jayne, you sound frightened. What can I do to help? Would you and Tom like me to go along? I'll be glad to. I don't even have to pack; my suitcase is still in the car."

"You're an absolute angel, Katie. We'd be so pleased to have you with us."

"Okay, Jayne. I'll call and make reservations for the flight you're scheduled on. I'm sure my mom will be able to drive us to the airport. We'll be at your house by seven o'clock."

"Thanks, Katie. I feel calmer just knowing you'll be along. See you soon."

Jayne said her goodbyes at work and notified her department co-workers that she would be away indefinitely. Friends and more co-workers offered words of encouragement all along the corridors as she hurried out, and Jayne promised to keep them posted on Nicholas' progress. Just as she exited the hospital doors, an irony struck her: Nicholas had been born at this very place where today she'd received word he would be getting a new heart—a new chance for a long life.

The night had grown chilly, and the Friday traffic seemed perversely heavy as she drove to pick up Nicholas at his grandma's house. The "Academy Award Performance," as it is now referred to, that she put on for Nicholas and Grandma Alice went without a hitch.

"Wasn't it lucky," she said, "that work was slow and I could get the night off?" She gathered Nicholas' toys and bundled him up, never faltering in her high energy and excitement. "Let's give Grandma a big hug and kiss goodbye, Nicholas. We love our Grandma Alice so much!"

As she handed Nicholas to Tom's mom for hugs and kisses, Jayne's eyes misted. *Please, Lord, don't let this precious boy die in surgery tonight.*

Grandma returned Nicholas to his mother's arms and Jayne kissed her mother-in-law goodbye, saying, "We *all* love you, Mom, very much. We'll call you tomorrow."

They arrived home minutes before Tom, and Jayne quickly began to pack. Clothes for Tom and herself. A warm blanket, books, and toys for Nicholas. Quick calls were made to cancel upcoming appointments and to arrange for neighbors to water the lawn and take care of Kipling. Nicholas played contentedly in his crib, turning the pages of his books and talking to his little plastic Kermit doll. Katie and her mom arrived as our suitcases were

slamming shut. Tom packed our things into their car . . . and off
we went to the airport. We were alternately quiet with introspec-
tion, and boisterous with the spirit of an adventure begun.

Nicholas laughed and clapped his hands with delight as we sat
in the waiting area at the airline departure gate. For his sake, we
were all keeping up the pretense of "this is just another night in
the life of the Millers."

We boarded the plane and Nicholas sat very quietly on his
daddy's lap. As we took off, his eyes grew big as saucers; he held
on tight as Tom hugged him to himself. Once airborne, Nicholas
grew fussy from hunger. He looked expectantly all around. Food
was his due by then—he knew that perfectly well—so he looked
for a bottle or a cracker or anything. Jayne brought out a pacifier,
something he hadn't even seen since he was three months old. He
put it into his mouth and sucked eagerly for a moment. Then,
realizing that there was no refreshment forthcoming, he pulled it
out of his mouth, looked at it with scorn, and promptly dropped
it in Jayne's lap. She gave him a small chip off an ice cube, which
soothed him temporarily. Katie then offered to hold him, and she
read to him for a few minutes. Fortunately the flight lasted only
an hour. Once on the ground, we rented a car with a child's car
seat and soon our little traveler fell off to sleep.

We arrived at Loma Linda University Medical Center at midnight. The transplant coordinator, Cheri Mathis, and the social
worker, Sherrianne Okawa, were waiting in the lobby to greet us.
Both wore white lab coats, but there the resemblance between
them ended. Cheri was fair, with shoulder-length golden-blond
hair; she wore braces that sparkled in the lobby light. Sherrianne
was dark and had very long, straight black hair. They were obviously tired, but they smiled broadly in welcome.

After introductions Cheri said, "We were just sitting here talking, wondering what you'd be like."

Jayne said, "Did we fulfill your expectations?"

"Oh, yes," said Sherrianne, and our two guides exchanged
glances and giggled good-humoredly. They led us into the elevator. As the doors began to close, the elevator said, "Going up."

We looked around, startled, and Cheri said, "Oh, you'll get used to these elevators. They announce all the stops. Aren't they funny?"

"Seventh floor," said the elevator in a metallic, computer-generated voice. The doors opened, and we all chuckled at the wonders of technology.

We walked down a long, door-lined corridor. Faintly in the background, we heard the elevator say, "Going down." Cheri explained, "Dr. Bailey is on his way in to talk with you and answer all your questions. Please be frank with him and let him know your concerns. He's very easy to work with."

We entered Unit 7100 and were taken to Nicholas' admitting room, where large murals of playful cartoon ducks and turtles hung on the walls. We continued to get acquainted with the staff until, moments later, Dr. Bailey arrived. Tall, lean, and casually attired in a pastel sportshirt, he introduced himself and invited us to sit down. The first thing we noticed about Dr. Bailey, besides his thick, prematurely gray hair, was the compassion in his eyes. Squinting with concern, those eyes really looked *at* us when he spoke. Even before he uttered a word, we could feel his care and empathy.

He described the proposed procedure, speaking quietly and calmly, and then stressed the need for a transplant: "Your boy has a very large heart that doesn't pump very efficiently. It's a condition that simply cannot reverse itself. His recent bout of pneumonia and congestive heart failure showed us just how little cardiac reserve he has. You can expect that sort of thing to happen more often. A heart transplant would give this boy a chance—a new healthy heart to replace his diseased one."

Tom, who held Nicholas against his shoulder, said, "Dr. Bailey, you can see that this little boy doesn't *look* sick. Except at the very beginning, and recently with pneumonia, he's *never* looked sick. Can you explain this?"

"Apparently he's been well compensated by his medicines. But you can't expect that to continue indefinitely. His last illness proves that."

"This is such an important decision for us," Tom said hopelessly. "If we choose to go ahead with it, when will you need to operate?"

"We plan to go over to Los Angeles to pick up the heart first thing in the morning. We'll leave here around six. If you decide to proceed, we'll have to do some tests—blood panels, chest X-rays, an electrocardiogram, and the like. We'll also have to give Nicholas a loading dose of cyclosporine—the main antirejection medicine. And to make sure he gets it all, we'll have to pass a small tube down his nose into his stomach."

"Is that how he'll always have to get this drug?" Jayne questioned, for once on totally new ground.

"Oh, no, usually he'll just drink it down with a chaser of chocolate milk. Tonight, though, he must get a large dose, and we want it to be absorbed fully, so we want to make sure it goes straight into his tummy. You should know that it's likely Nicholas will be on this medicine for the rest of his life."

Jayne interrupted: "What about side effects, doctor? We've read that cyclosporine caused kidney damage in Baby Fae."

"It's true that cyclosporine can cause kidney problems, so we watch blood levels very closely and give the least amount of the drug to do the job of preventing rejection without damaging the kidneys."

"Where does the drug come from, Doctor?" asked Tom.

"Cyclosporine comes from a fungus found only in Switzerland. Then it's suspended in an oily base that prevents spoilage. It's revolutionized transplantation, because it really does fight rejection. We balance it with another medicine called Imuran. Though rejection episodes will occur, we can treat and control them with these and other medicines more effectively than ever. The survival rate of adult heart transplant patients is about 70 percent now."

"But heart transplantation is still experimental in babies and children as young as Nicholas?" Tom asked. "That's something we have to bear in mind?"

"Yes, that's true."

"And the first infant transplant—Baby Moses, I believe—has survived for six months, is that correct?"

"Yes, he's doing quite well, as is Baby Eve, whom we operated on not long after Moses."

Holding his son tightly to his chest, Tom looked hard at Jayne. Nicholas, sensing something important, was alert but quiet.

"It's so hard," Tom said.

Dr. Bailey was quiet himself for a long moment. Then he said, "I have two sons of my own—also adopted—so I know how important Nicholas is to you. But I can only imagine what a difficult decision this is for you. You should both know that there is no *wrong* decision. If you decide to walk out of here and go home, we'll understand and respect that. We won't think any less of you. He's your boy. *You* have to decide what's best for your boy."

At that moment, two thoughts came to Tom's mind with equal weight. The first was a memory of Doyle, our cherished gray tabby who died of a heart murmur at the age of seven during the Christmas season of 1984. Three separate veterinarians had told us over four years that, despite Doyle's healthy appearance, we were bound to lose him soon. And in fact we did.

The second thought was of Nicholas when we tried to discontinue his quinidine. Our cheerful, perfect-looking little boy played normally in his hospital crib, while the nearby monitor clearly showed his heart beating dangerously—showed the double, triple, and quadruple irregular beats that could easily lead to fibrillation and . . .

Tom couldn't even think the word. It was plain that appearances meant nothing—that when doctors said a heart was bound to fail, they meant what they said.

Once again he asked himself, *Is there even a choice?*

At that moment, Tom made up his mind. *No, there isn't a choice.*

Dr. Bailey was still talking: "I need to know your answer in the next hour so that, should you decide to proceed, I can get tests ordered and we can all be ready to go by six. In that event, Nicholas will go down to the operating room at about eight. You can be with him right up until that time."

We offered our thanks to Dr. Bailey for his candor and his time. Then we were shown to an empty room where we could make our final decision together in privacy. Katie stayed behind, rocking a sleepy Nicholas.

We sat at a table and held hands. We were surrounded by bare walls. Tom said, "What do you think?"

"I think we should let him have the surgery, darling. I trust Dr. Bailey. He seems so sincere and kind. Just the fact that he'd take time to explain the procedure and field our questions is an indication of how sincere and dedicated he is. Believe me, most surgeons of his stature wouldn't give us the time of day."

"I know," said Tom.

"Another thing that helps me is that only a few days ago we took Nicholas to see Fr. Bain. He prayed that Nicholas' heart would be 'renewed and transformed,' and it seems tonight that our prayers have really been answered. I believe that we as a family have been guided here tonight."

"You're right, angel; I believe that, too. But still, what if Nicholas dies? What will we *do* if we lose him?"

"Tommy," Jayne said, our hands squeezing together tightly, "if we're meant to lose Nicholas, somewhere we'll find the strength to accept that. I really have a good feeling about this, though—that he's going to be okay."

Tom was quiet for a while, lost in his thoughts. Then he said, "You know, Jayne, I'm very proud to be Nicholas' daddy. He's such a brave little boy; he's gone through so much, and yet he always seems so happy. You know what? Being his daddy makes me feel important. He needs me. He needs *us*. We've been good parents. What would we do without him?"

Again tightening her grip on his hands, Jayne said, "Darling, *we* have to be brave now. We have to be brave for all three of us. There isn't even really a decision to be made. We have to go through with it—for Nicholas' sake."

"I believe that *with all my heart,*" Tom said. "I *do,* but it's so hard."

He looked deep into Jayne's eyes. "If we lose him, Jayne, I can't handle a big funeral with a casket and everything, okay? I can't bear the thought of having to keep together in front of all those people, when I'll probably feel like rolling into a comatose ball. You come from a big family. All the funerals in your family are always so *big* and *formal.* Promise me it will be quiet and simple?"

"I promise."

We spent a moment more discussing funeral arrangements, in case the need should arise. And then, knowing that we had mentally prepared ourselves, we stood up.

It was a dreadful moment.

We held one another tightly and Jayne murmured, "I believe we're doing the right thing. We're giving Nicholas every possible chance for a long life."

"I know, I know. Let's go see our little guy and tell Dr. Bailey."

Seeing the doctor bent over a chart at the nursing station, we approached him. Tom said, "Well, Dr. Bailey, as far as I'm concerned, when you do the operation, your hands are the hands of God."

Dr. Bailey's eyes squinted at us as he smiled and said, "We'll do our best." He then handed Tom a form, saying, "This is a consent form allowing us to perform the surgery. It needs one of your signatures."

Tom studied the sheet for a moment, then picked up a nearby pen and slowly signed the paper. He looked it over once more, then handed the pen to Jayne.

A clerk at the nursing station piped in, "Oh, only one of you needs to sign it."

"That's okay," Jayne said, affixing her signature. In our minds it was clear that an authorization of this magnitude required both our signatures—if only to symbolize that we had made this most crucial decision together and that we took equal responsibility.

We all shook hands and Dr. Bailey assured us that he'd give us a full report after the surgery.

We left and rejoined our son in his room. He was asleep in

Katie's arms. He stirred when he heard our whispered voices and reached out for Mommy. Jayne held her little boy close and her eyes began to sting. She said a quiet prayer: "Please, Lord, let this little boy fully recover. We love him so very much and want to watch him grow up."

The night nurse came in, quickly followed by Cheri and Sherrianne. Cheri explained the several procedures that would need to be done on Nicholas and said that we were welcome to stay with him. The night nurse was pleasant, and Nicholas warmed to her immediately. She changed him into a little yellow patient gown and weighed and measured him. He weighed two pounds less than he had at his twelve-month checkup. Jayne knew that this weight loss was a subtle sign of cardiac deterioration. As his vital signs were being taken, Sherrianne told us that the Medical Center would provide housing for us for as long as Nicholas remained hospitalized. She then took Katie to a small efficiency studio apartment two blocks away and showed her where the soap, towels, and linen were kept so that we could settle in right away.

To say that we were grateful is an understatement. Imagine these fine people agreeing to operate on our son at no charge to us and then giving us temporary lodging as well! Though we had only just met, we already felt that we were among friends.

The next two hours were frantic, with one procedure after another. Nicholas weathered the EKG, chest X-ray, and blood test like an old trooper.

But slipping the feeding tube down his nose was something else entirely. Nicholas was already lying on his back. The nurse picked up the tube, which wasn't quite as thick as a soda straw. As she brought it up to Nicholas' face, he turned his head and reached up for it.

Jayne said, "Perhaps I can help."

"That would be fine. If you held his arms down?" Jayne did as she was told, thinking—mistakenly, as it turned out—that her presence would reassure her son.

The night nurse tried to hold Nicholas' head still with one hand while trying to get the tube into a nostril with the other. But Nicholas proved too much of a fighter.

She called out to another nurse, "Please come hold his head."

The second nurse stepped over, then held on for all she was worth as the night nurse aimed the tube. Finally she managed to slip it in partially, with Nicholas kicking and screaming. He truly *screamed* for the first time in his life. His eyes bulged wide with terror. He simply couldn't understand. All the while, Jayne held on tightly, trying to encourage him along. His struggles dislodged the tube, and they had to start again.

Not able to watch his son endure such horrible fear, and feeling more totally helpless than he ever had, Tom stood off to the side, his fists clenched white. He grimaced until his jaw hurt, and he sobbed . . . and sobbed. Katie came to his side and slowly drew him out of the room into the hallway.

"Katie, it's so hard," he gasped. "Why does this have to happen? My son's in there scared out of his mind, and there's nothing I can do!" His back was against a wall, Katie facing him. She placed both her hands firmly on his shoulders. "It's the hardest thing I've ever endured," he said, his voice rising.

"We don't have all the answers, Tom," Katie said. She looked up into his eyes, and he could see that she needed him to collect himself. "We can only do the best we can. I know watching Nicholas like this hurts. It hurts awfully. But it has to be done. The procedure is important."

All the while, as her own heart broke, Jayne beseeched over and over, *Please, Lord, if this is this child's last night of life, don't let it be this way.*

After seven attempts, the tube finally went down and the medicine was promptly administered. Nicholas got lots of hugs from Mommy and he calmed down quickly. Uttering sighs of exhaustion, he fell right to sleep on her shoulder.

Tom and Katie returned to the room. After a while, he suggested that Katie should show Jayne the apartment, and that the two women should shower and sleep for the rest of the night. After they had left, Tom settled into a rocking chair with his son. Nicholas slept peacefully in his arms for the next two hours. The room was quiet now, and the lights were dimmed. There was only a father holding his bushy-haired little boy close, trying to protect him, but exhausted and confused himself. The clock read three-thirty in the morning. A nurse stepped quietly in and covered them both with a blanket. Time moved slowly.

Tom was frightened. But he had complete faith in God. If we weren't doing the right thing, why on earth would God have given us this awesome gift just days after Fr. Bain had asked the Lord for Nicholas' heart to be renewed?

In this meditative frame of mind, Tom allowed his thoughts to wander backward. He remembered that remarkable fortune he'd received in a cookie just hours after Nicholas was born: *You are the guiding star of his existence.* He glowed inside with the memory. *Such a responsibility,* he thought. He gazed down at his son's face and lightly stroked his long dark curls. *May your existence be long, my son, so your mom and I can guide you far.*

His mind roamed further back—to late 1979, to the warmth of another cherished memory. We were busy putting postage on our wedding invitations. The stamps pictured a rose in full bloom, and because Rose was Jayne's maiden name, we felt that this was a nice touch. Tom joked, "All we need now is a stamp with a windmill to use on the thank-you notes"—his thought being that the windmill would represent his family name, Miller. No sooner had we returned from our honeymoon than we discovered that the Post Office *had* just issued a series of windmill stamps. We were so impressed—for it was as if God had affirmed our union—that we juxtaposed two book pages of these stamps in an oak frame, hoping that our children would someday think of them as a family heirloom.

With this thought, Tom pressed his son closer. Nicholas stirred, smacked his lips sleepily, opened his eyes for a second, then settled back down.

Two nurses began talking outside the room. They moved off, and as the sound of their voices faded away, Tom remembered another incident—one so special and private that he'd never shared it with anyone, not even Jayne. As he held his son close, he thought back twenty months—six months before Nicholas' birth.

It seemed such a simple thing that he hadn't thought much about it at the time. He'd been running errands on California Street in Palo Alto—as it happened, only a quarter-block from where we'd had our wedding rings made. Just as he stepped off the sidewalk to cross the street, a car passed him, and he noticed that the three letters in the license plate spelled a word—VOW. He noticed it because he frequently passed time when stuck in commute traffic by trying to figure out the odd spellings and strange configurations people came up with for personalized license plates. It took him just a second to cross the street, and the first thing he noticed on the other side was a book displayed in a bookstore window. Its stark black cover bore a simple title in white letters, *The Miracle.* It was a new best-selling novel. He didn't think anything of it at the time, as he went about finishing his errands. Later in the day, he thought of the incident again, and the more he thought about it, the more the chance juxtaposition of *vow* and *miracle* nagged at his mind. It seemed like a message. As the days and weeks passed, he held this secret in his mind, and it became a small obsession. He'd daydream, *Okay, if we're going to have a miracle happen in our lives, what form would I like it to take?* He dreamed of having his novel accepted by a publisher, or of getting an offer for a perfect job. Then he thought that maybe it meant we'd find a baby. Isn't birth a miracle? For six months, he toyed with these kinds of thoughts.

And then Nicholas had come into our lives, and all the experiences that followed. Never had the world been so intense or chaotic. There was no room for daydreams in that world. It was all we could do just to fight for survival. Then one day, in a meeting, the chief physician of Stanford's ICN called Nicholas' survival a miracle—an AFM!

Tom hadn't known what to think. He'd forgotten about his little obsession in the twists and turns and slamming trap doors of those previous five weeks. But now he remembered. God had vowed a miracle. Little had Tom known what form it would take.

꿍

Rocking his treasured son, his little boy's head lying trustingly on his shoulder, Tom sighed and returned to the present. He was more afraid than he'd ever been in his life. Yet he believed in his heart of hearts, as Jayne did, that they'd been *guided* to Loma Linda that night. Just as Nicholas relied on him and Jayne, Tom knew he himself had to rely on God.

He closed his eyes and began to pray the Lord's Prayer in a whisper. When he reached "Thy will be done," he stopped. The hospital was warm and eerily quiet, except for the telltale sound of the furnace. He thought about the four words he'd just spoken.

"God," he asked quietly, "what *is* your will? Already you've shown us that your will is far different, far more awesome, than any of the petty things we can imagine. What is your will for us?"

He didn't expect an answer. He just held Nicholas tightly, knowing, trusting that they were doing the right thing, and tried to banish any further thoughts from his mind. He closed his eyes, feeling his son's warm body snuggled up to him, and tried to rest himself.

꿍

At a quarter to six, Jayne and Katie returned and sent Tom off to shower and shave. An hour later we were all together in Nicholas' room, where we sang songs and clapped our hands. Nicholas joined in vigorously, despite an IV and armboard taped to his right hand. We played peekaboo, and, for the first time ever, Nicholas took the blanket off his own head and put it over Mommy's head and laughed. Jayne's heart filled—grateful for such a wonderful memory only moments before Nicholas was to go to the O.R.

Katie took pictures of the Miller family, and Nicholas grinned excitedly. He knew that a camera meant smiles, and he'd begun months before to pose and grin as soon as he saw a lens. The moment was a wonderful time of family togetherness.

At seven-fifty a quiet, natty man with silver hair and a mustache to match entered the room. Nicholas sat on Tom's lap as the man approached and introduced himself. "Mr. and Mrs. Miller, I'm Bill Hinton. I'm one of the Adventist ministers from the chaplaincy service here at Loma Linda. I've been trying to contact a Catholic priest to come and offer support and prayer for you folks, as you had requested. Unfortunately our Catholic chaplain is away at a conference, and the priests at the Veterans' Hospital are unavailable. I want you to know, however, that I'm available to offer prayers with you for your baby son and for the success of his surgery. The social workers and I will also be with you throughout the day, keeping you updated on how your baby's surgery is progressing."

Bill asked us to join him in a circle. Then we were led in prayer by this kind and gentle man, who in days to come would become our trusted and dear friend.

One of the nurses came in and told us that Dr. Bailey and his team had arrived at the L.A. hospital and were in the process of recovering the donor heart.

We continued to hold Nicholas on our laps and play "Where's Mommy?" and "Where's Daddy?" as the time quickly approached eight o'clock. All too soon, the nurse returned to tell us that we could all walk down to the operating room together now.

Tom carried Nicholas, who busied himself looking around. He appeared aware that something was about to happen. Though we all tried to look calm, Jayne heard her own heart beating loudly and thought, *Can this really be happening?* She looked constantly at Nicholas' face and hands, wanting to memorize every detail of them should she never see her son alive again.

We left Unit 7100 and slowly walked down the hallway, turning right toward the elevators. Jayne, Tom, Nicholas, Katie, Bill Hinton, and two nurses—a small band of people moving toward an unknown future for our family. Jayne stayed close to Tom, close to Nicholas. Hope and hopelessness became one. Out of sheer self-defense, numbness took hold.

The nurse pushed the second-floor button in the elevator. "Going down," said the metallic voice as the doors shut and our stomachs sank. A moment later, the voice said, "Second floor."

The doors opened. We stepped forward as if in a trance. Bill and the nurses led us down another hall. Jayne noticed that the floor was white linoleum speckled with brown. This hall, too, was lined with doors. We turned a corner and stopped in front of a set of wide double doors. The operating suite.

At the same moment, a priest from the nearby Veterans' Hospital came running down the hall, breathless but intent on anointing our son. He led us all in the Lord's Prayer, then, as quickly as he had arrived, he hurried off.

The double doors swung open, and the chief anesthesiologist and a senior resident, who had come to check on Nicholas earlier, appeared. A nurse handed Jayne a paper showercap to place over Nicholas' dark curls. She did so, and Nicholas squirmed from Tom's arms into her own. She hugged her little boy close, feeling the now-familiar stinging in her eyes. "I love you, little Nicholas, more than you may ever know. I love you, my son." Nicholas pulled away and looked at Jayne as if to say, "Why are you so serious, Mommy?"

She rubbed her cheek against the sweet softness of his and handed him back to his misty-eyed daddy.

Tom looked into his son's eyes, brushed a curl off his forehead, and said, as he did every night when he put him to bed, "May God protect you, my son." He held him tightly one last time. "I love you so much, Nicholas."

Knowing the difficulty of the moment, the resident said brightly, "I have children, and I'll take care of Baby James as if he were one of my own." He then took Nicholas from Tom's arms and gave our son a kiss on the crown of his head. Off they went like two old friends.

The chief anesthesiologist quickly began asking us questions about allergies and medications. Tom answered them, but we both kept our eyes riveted on the image of our son in the arms of the doctor walking down the long hall of the operating suite. Jayne wanted to run through the slowly closing double doors and yell, "I've changed my mind: he's not going through with it." She instead kept her feet firmly planted on the floor, took a deep breath, and tried hard to pay attention as the doctor spoke to us.

But our eyes stayed on our son until the doors closed completely and there was nothing more to see.

Chapter Eleven

"I bet you haven't had a bite to eat in hours," Bill Hinton said, gently turning us away from the doors. "Why don't we all go down to the cafeteria and have some breakfast?"

On the way, he detoured us into the chaplain's office and led us in prayer once more. We were grateful for his presence, his attentiveness, and his understanding.

"Now don't forget, you'll be updated periodically from the operating room. You'll be able to wait here in my office, and they'll phone up every few minutes."

Shock had settled in. We went where Bill led us. In a few minutes, we found ourselves in the cafeteria, waiting in line to be served. Tom looked at the clock on the beige wall. It was eight-thirty on a Saturday morning—Sabbath for the Seventh-day Adventists, whose motto for their hospital is "To Make Man Whole."

We sat at a table in the largely empty cafeteria and pondered the food, which was entirely vegetarian—even the ham and sausage links, which were soy-based look-alikes. Tom looked for pepper for his eggs.

"Oh, you won't find any pepper here," Bill said, smiling. "Our church frowns on its use."

"Why on earth?" came Tom's astonished reply.

"One of our early leaders, Ellen G. White, was concerned about its untoward effects on the body."

There followed a brief discussion of the pros and cons of salt, pepper, and seasoned salt, which appeared prominently on all the tables in place of pepper.

Bill couldn't have been more congenial. He knew what must be going through our minds and hearts, and tried to keep our spirits up.

After a long lull, Tom said, "I wish we knew more about the donor. It seems so strange being the recipient of such a wonderful gift and knowing nothing about the giver."

"Oh? It's been all over the papers the last few days. What do you know?"

"Only that Dr. Bailey said the donor is an eighteen-month-old girl and that she died as the result of some 'inner-city drama.' "

"You know," Bill said, "there was something on the news last night. There's probably something in this morning's papers, too. It was a Thorazine overdose, I think."

At the other end of the table were a couple of newspapers left by earlier diners. Bill grabbed these and began flipping through the pages of the *Los Angeles Times.* "Here it is." He slid the section across the table, and we gazed in wonder and apprehension at the headline.

MAN CLEARED OF ABUSE
DONATES GIRL'S ORGANS

The article began, "A grief-stricken Los Angeles man, mistakenly accused of child abuse earlier this week, gave doctors permission on Friday to disconnect his brain-dead eighteen-month-old daughter from life-support systems and make her heart and other organs available for transplantation."

It went on to say that the man, a recent widower, had brought his sick baby into a downtown L.A. hospital, telling doctors that he believed the girl had swallowed some Thorazine that she'd found in a dresser drawer. Because of "suspicious circumstances," police had charged him with child abuse and taken him into custody. Even after determining that there was no reason to prosecute, police had continued to hold the man for outstanding minor offenses, such as traffic violations.

As we finished reading, Bill showed us a similar article in the *San Bernardino Sun.* "It's a sad case," he said.

"I can't believe that they could keep the man in jail as long as they did," Jayne said. "My God, his child was dying! Couldn't they have had *any* compassion?"

Tom reached out and took Jayne's hands, knowing that our thoughts once again meshed: *Jesus, help this poor man. His little daughter has died. But in so doing, she made it possible that our son will live. Lord, please give your strength to us all.*

◄§

By nine we were back in Bill's office, where Sherrianne was waiting for us. She asked us, "Would you like something—juice or water?" Bill left the room to call the operating room. He returned in a few minutes.

"The donor heart has been recovered successfully. It's in transport now and is one hour away. Your son's been prepared, anesthesia's been given, and everything is coming along fine."

Bill and Sherrianne both sat in chairs in front of us. With Katie, there were five of us in the small office. After a while, we ran out of things to say, and though Tom knew that Bill and Sherrianne didn't want to leave us alone at this critical time, he felt the strong need to be alone with his wife and friend. Eventually he said, "Bill, Sherrianne, would you mind if we were alone for a while?"

"No, not at all. We'll be in the office two doors down if you need us."

After they left, Katie leaned over to Jayne and said something in a hushed voice; then they both broke into hysterical laughter. Tom looked at them, bewildered.

"Oh, Tommy, Katie and I are just releasing the tension, I guess," Jayne said. "You know how we can communicate almost without words because we've known one another so long." Tom smiled, but soberly. A half-hour went by; then Bill knocked on the door and poked his head in. He said, "The donor heart is ten minutes away. Your son is doing fine."

Jayne and Katie chatted, and the minutes crept by.

Another knock: "The heart is here. They're getting ready to make the first incision in Baby James."

A half-hour later, at ten-fifty, Bill came in. "Dr. Bailey has made the first incision. Your son is doing very well."

After having sat in the office for an hour and a half, our nerves frayed with the mounting pressure, we decided that we had to get some air.

At Bill's suggestion, we went to the Day Room, where we'd be near a phone. He would alert the O.R. where to find us. Because the Day Room was jammed with patients and visitors watching TV, we passed through its smoky stuffiness out onto the patio solarium. The sun shone brightly through a hazy sky, and the breeze felt refreshing. We three moved around in a state of shock, chatting about anything that crossed our minds, our ears alert for the sound of the telephone ringing inside.

At eleven-thirty it rang, and Jayne rushed to answer it.

"Is this Mrs. James?"

"Ah . . . this is Baby James' mother, yes."

"Your son's heart has been removed, and the new heart is being sutured into place. He's doing just fine."

"Thank you. Thank you so very much!"

She turned to Tom, who hovered close to her shoulder, and repeated the news. We held hands as we went back to meet Katie out on the patio.

"I can't believe this. I've never known another hospital to give regular updates like this. Can you imagine what it would be like if we knew *nothing* and had to wait for hours? And that's the way most hospitals treat the family. I'm so impressed!"

Five minutes later, Bill and Sherrianne came in.

"It took only thirty-three minutes to make the exchange," Bill said. "Amazing, isn't it—a complicated procedure like this in only a half-hour? You can rest assured that Dr. Bailey is the best."

Ten minutes later, the phone rang again.

"The new heart is completely sutured in and beating slowly," came the nurse's voice at the other end. "They'll begin warming Baby James now." This was a reference to the surgery having been performed while Nicholas' core body temperature was kept cold. "They'll raise his temperature slowly in the next hour."

At one-twenty they called again. "Baby James is doing well. He's off the heart/lung bypass. Would you like to hear his heart beating?"

"Of course!" Jayne could hardly believe this.

The nurse held the receiver to the oscilloscope, and at our end we both had our ears crammed to the phone.

"Beep . . . beep . . . beep . . . beep . . . beep . . . beep." It was thrilling!

"We'll let him warm up a bit more, then close him up and return him to the seventh floor, where a special sterile room has been made ready."

A half-hour later, at two o'clock, Bill suggested that we should meet with Dick Schaefer, the director of community relations. He was getting ready to write a press release and needed our input so that the press would be told only what we wanted it to know. Bill took the three of us back down to Dick's office and introduced us, then left.

His beard beginning to be speckled with white, Dick was soft-spoken and alert to everything we had to say. In shirt, tie, and sportcoat, he sat behind his desk with a small word processor on his lap.

"The press is beginning to wonder what became of the donated heart. The case has been in the news for almost a week, you know, and they've heard rumors that Loma Linda received the heart; but our policy is not to divulge information about donors or their families. It's in the hospital's best interest, however, to release that we've done your son's transplant. But let me explain your rights and options.

"We can do just about anything that you want to do. We can report nothing at all, if that's your wish. However, there's a high probability that that would only get the press wondering what the secrecy is about and be counterproductive in the long run. Or you can choose to report everything—your names and the full details of your life. Or you can choose some point between those extremes."

"We've discussed this already," Jayne said, "and we've decided that we need to protect Nicholas, as well as our own privacy. But to help alert people to your program and to the need for donor hearts, we'll allow the fact of the surgery to be reported, *but nothing more*—no names, photos, or any details. After all, we ourselves wouldn't have known about Dr. Bailey's work if the media hadn't reported it so vigorously—especially Baby Fae."

Dick jotted down a couple of notes on a blank pad. "I think that's the most reasonable route to take. At this point in your lives, the last thing you need is a media circus."

"That's true," said Tom. "But there are other factors that make it important that our identities stay out of the press. You see, Nicholas is adopted. That in itself could be considered a 'juicy detail,' journalistically speaking, and on top of all the other press this heart and the donor have gotten—'inner-city drama' and all— we might be in for some really rough times if that fact became known. On top of that, we've never met his birthparents, so we have no idea if he's the perfect image of one or another or both of them. We have no idea what kind of people they or their relatives are. We have no idea what they would do or how they would react if they saw their child or grandchild suddenly all over the newspapers. It's simply best all around and will cause us less worry if nothing but the fact of the surgery is reported."

Jayne spoke again. "But we would also like to thank the donor family—"

The phone rang. Dick answered it and murmured a few words, then hung up.

"That was a reporter from the *Los Angeles Times* wanting confirmation that the little girl's heart had come here. Apparently the L.A. hospital has made a statement already. I said only that we were working on a press release that would be ready this afternoon."

The phone rang again.

"That was UPI. They wanted to interview the recipient's parents, and I told them the same thing."

With Dick's help, we began to piece together the announcement. After listening to everything we had to say and offering his responses, he typed a few lines on his little laptop.

"How about this for a beginning? 'A fourteen-month-old northern California boy, named Baby James—' "

Tom screwed up his face. "Well, he *is* fourteen months old, but from that his approximate birthdate could be calculated, and combining that with 'northern California,' we might be giving away more than we want."

Dick thought for a minute, then made some corrections. "How about this?" He read the new version, and so it went. The finished press release comprised only four short paragraphs, but it took all of two hours to write because of our insistence that no detail could be traceable back to us and because we were interrupted by at least fifteen phone calls from the local and national media.

The completed press release said, in part:

April 26, 1986

A fifteen-month-old California boy, named Baby James, underwent a successful human-to-human heart transplant at Loma Linda University Medical Center this afternoon. . . .

Baby James had suffered from cardiomyopathy, a general deterioration of the heart muscle. . . .

The parents of Baby James have expressed gratitude to the donor family for the difficult decision they made and for the gift of life to Baby James.

In harmony with the parents' wishes, future additional information beyond this statement will be released at their discretion. . . .

As we completed the statement at three-thirty, Cheri Mathis poked her head in to say that Nicholas had been taken up to his room. Then, just as the final press release slid out of Dick's office printer, Dr. Bailey came in, still wearing scrubs, a yellow gown, and paper shoe covers. He seemed a little shy and uncomfortable as he stood with his back to the door, explaining the details of Nicholas' condition, summarizing by saying, "Nicholas is a brave boy. He seems to be doing very well. I'm cautiously optimistic."

What a relief it was to hear those words!

All at once, the doctor brought his right hand out from behind his back. The hand held a quart jar. "This is your son's heart," he said. "I thought you'd be interested in seeing it."

Knowing Jayne to be a hospital employee, and knowing that we were concerned not only about our son's condition but also about our decision on his behalf, he didn't hesitate to show us the heart that had been keeping our little boy alive—but just barely.

Astounded, Jayne took the jar of formaldehyde solution and we examined the organ inside. The pink muscle was almost hidden by a basketweave of white scar tissue.

"It looks almost like tripe," Jayne said, staring hard.

"There's no doubt in my mind that we did the right thing," Dr. Bailey said. "With all our experience with cardiomyopathy, we know that this heart couldn't have lasted much longer. The left ventricle muscle should be at least five times thicker than what you see there. The extensive scar tissue is a result of the initial viral episode."

In awe that we were holding our son's heart in our hands, we examined every facet of it. Jayne turned the jar slowly, pointing out details she noticed, then handed it to Tom. He held it at every possible angle, peering through the glass, asking questions. "Which is the left ventricle?" "If this is grossly enlarged, what size should it have been?"

When we had seen all there was to see and all our questions were answered, Tom set the jar down on Dick's dark wooden desk. It stood there in mute testimony to the miracles that humankind itself had learned to perform. Now our son was the recipient of two miracles. One God-given, the other given by a man but apparently blessed by God.

Profoundly overwhelmed, we looked at one another, hardly believing that any of this could be happening. How many parents get to gauge their child's health in terms of miracles? How many parents have the opportunity to hold their child's heart in their hands? *Our* child, who was "doing very well" despite the fact that the heart he was born with was no longer pumping inside him.

We looked up at Dr. Bailey. "Thank you so much for sharing this with us," Jayne said. "It helps us to know that we did the right thing." It seemed such an anemic response, but she meant it from the depths of her soul. What else *could* she say? Then her thoughts focused on her little boy, and she heard her husband ask the most important question of all.

"Doctor, when can we see Nicholas?"

"Why don't you wait about a half-hour, then you can go up and gown and scrub." He winked and left, taking the jar with him.

The shock of the whole experience and our lack of sleep were beginning to take their toll. We felt we were sleepwalking. When we looked into one another's eyes, we stared into bottomless pools.

We said thank you to Dick for his kind help, then slowly made our way up to the seventh floor. Katie couldn't go into Nicholas' room with us, so we dropped her off at the Day Room. In our hearts, we knew that this whole experience would have been infinitely more difficult if she hadn't been there for us. Thankful that we were blessed to have such a friend, we went on to the nursing station. A nurse showed us where to scrub for three minutes, and we put on fresh gowns, shoe covers, and masks.

Then—finally—we stepped through one set of double doors and then through another into Nicholas' room.

Attended by a nurse and a respiratory therapist, there lay our son—sedated and pale, breathing with the aid of a respirator.

But alive!

Despite the maze of tubes and lines, he looked peaceful, and we'd been told that he was stable. We couldn't hold him yet, so we stood as close as we could, stroking his face and his thick, curly hair, grasping tightly his little hands in ours.

We cried. Oh, we cried—and said a prayer, thanking God for this newest miracle in the life of our brave little boy, Nicholas Lawrence Miller.

Chapter Twelve

The Medical Center discharged Nicholas eighteen days later. His recovery following surgery had been swift and uneventful. He had quickly regained his natural cheerfulness and activity level and showed no signs of being a postoperative patient. The only reminder that he had undergone major surgery was a pencil-thin incision line extending along his breastbone five inches down his chest. We called it his "zipper," and sometimes when we tickled him there, he'd run his fingers along its length and laugh.

Jayne took Nicholas "home" to the temporary lodging that the hospital had been providing and that we took to calling "the bungalow." This bungalow had a large concrete patio that Nicholas loved. He had learned to use a walker while in the hospital, and he enjoyed the sunshine on his face and the breeze he produced when scooting around at high speed. He'd chuckle and yelp at Mommy and be annoyed when they'd return to the confining indoors.

Tom had returned to work on May 15, a few days before Nicholas' release. After careful review, we'd decided that we couldn't chance our new-house loan being turned down because of his leave of absence. He had to return to work while Nicholas was still in the hospital. He would then begin a rigorous schedule of working in the Bay Area Monday through Friday and commuting by air to be with his family on the weekends.

The first weekend he devoted to moving his wife and son out of the bungalow into a nearby brand-new one-bedroom apartment. It seemed that he hardly had a chance to see them before he was back on the plane heading north.

Inside of a few hours, between toddling in his walker and a combination of crawling and walking while holding onto furniture, Nicholas had explored every inch of his new abode.

The day after Tom left, Nicholas' first signs of rejection were diagnosed. Dr. Bailey had anticipated this, as each transplant patient is expected to have two or three such episodes soon after the surgery. These episodes are closely monitored and vigorously treated with steroids. They're scary because they're the primary life-threatening complication of organ transplantation. One's own body is literally rejecting the new organ necessary for life.

Nicholas' antirejection treatment consisted of a seven-day course of steroid pills, given on a tapering schedule. The pills had to be crushed up and mixed into yogurt, fruit, or ice cream to conceal their extremely bitter flavor.

Nevertheless, Nicholas made great strides in development during this time. Playing with pots and pans from the kitchen cupboards delighted him, and he remained fascinated with hinges and the movement of the cupboard doors themselves.

He loved seeing colors emerge from a pen or crayon. He'd look up at his mom, eyes as big as saucers, showing astonishment as if magic had been performed.

And bubbles—bubbles lit him right up! He'd chuckle and point at them, following the pearly spheres with his eyes until—POP!— and then look at his mom with wonder.

Nicholas teethed during much of this time and awoke often during the night. His cries became screams, and he was very difficult to console. Other than giving him liquid Tylenol to quiet the pain, and holding and rocking him, there was nothing Jayne could do. Neither were the neighbors happy to have their sleep disrupted. But Jayne had no doubt that her usually happy child was reacting to the upheaval in his life, as well as to his painful gums.

During this period, Jayne took Nicholas to the many new housing developments around this rapidly growing area. Model homes were usually cleaned once a week and, with a quick phone call, she could find out what day and time. When that day arrived and the cleaning was all done, she'd pack Nicholas up and off they'd go for a free and fun adventure in a freshly cleaned environment.

One new subdivision had Cape Cod–style homes with perfectly appointed country interiors. Rich hues of hunter green and cranberry red, with camel and dark oak tones, set off the wing-back chairs and couches. Nicholas took one look around and yelped his approval. This looked like home! The decoy ducks and English hunt scenes made the house feel even more like the home he had known. The poor little imp thought he had returned to more comfortable surroundings.

He cried when he and his mom returned to the cramped apartment, furnished with modern motel-type couch, chair, and tables. Jayne, too, longed for her treasures, the homey comforts she wouldn't see again until she returned to northern California. It was hard to have one's life on hold, but she was grateful that Nicholas had survived. With a bit more time, according to our plan, normalcy would return.

The reality is that when a child receives an organ transplant, the entire family is transplanted. We now knew the pain of separation and relocation, the rigors of postop care, and the undercurrent of anxiety that the fear of rejection adds to each moment.

On top of everything else, we had many new and unforeseen bills to contend with. Thank goodness, Jayne's co-workers had generously donated part of their vacation time to her, so that we were still receiving her paycheck. Despite Tom's return to work, we were hanging on by a thread financially. But somehow we couldn't worry too much about that.

~§

Each day Jayne tried to add an additional decoration to increase Nicholas' visual stimulation—Mickey Mouse pictures, alphabet posters, and helium balloons floating at the ceiling. Photos of Nicholas and greeting cards from family and friends added to the collage being created on the walls. As Jayne added each new piece, they'd both clap with delight.

For exercise each day, Jayne put Nicholas in his stroller and pushed him along while she race-walked through the landscaped paths of the sprawling apartment complex. She'd avoid people on her route as much as possible, having learned that now, as ever, people gravitated to Nicholas and couldn't help pausing to chat.

Nicholas enjoyed these "high-speed" race-walk adventures. He'd throw his arms in the air and giggle and shriek like a thrill-seeking teenager on a rollercoaster. Clearly he was not timid. But he did look around often to make sure Mom was still there. His quizzical look would melt into a wide grin when he verified her presence and he'd return to his arms-up position, embracing the breeze.

It was important on these walks (and at all times) that Nicholas be kept from people who could possibly infect him. His post-transplant treatment consisted largely of *suppressing* his immune system to prevent his own body from rejecting the new heart. This meant that he was more susceptible than ever to other people's bugs.

Immediately post-transplant, Nicholas required nine new medications—a whole new regimen to replace the old. Following the instructions, remaining alert for side effects, administering the meds, and recording times given required more coordination and dedication than ever before. Jayne took vital signs twice a day—consisting of temperature, pulse with stethoscope, and respiration count. She recorded observations of his coloring and energy level, and documented food and liquid intake. When Tom was reunited with his family two or three days each week, he gladly took over these responsibilities.

Initially fluids were restricted, because excess water stored in body tissues would put an unnecessary strain on Nicholas' new heart. He enjoyed his milk, water, and juice and couldn't understand why we weren't as liberal with them as before. He'd hold his empty bottle up to us for a refill. Our job, despite the imploring look in his eyes, was to offer sufficient distraction to make him temporarily forget his thirst. When he awakened during the night back at home, a bottle normally put him right back to sleep. Now he awoke often at night, and the small amounts of liquid we could give him rarely satisfied.

For most of the week, the stresses of single parenthood with no respite mounted for Jayne. She loved her son and missed her husband. Nightly phone calls kept us going, and Jayne sent Tom cards and letters during the week. Despite all her attempts at positive thinking, she found herself suffering from cabin fever.

Though circumstances weren't exactly bleak, they took their toll. She'd been uprooted from her home and relocated to a strange environment, her career on hold, with no friends, no family—and solely responsible for a seriously ill child, despite appearances. She began to experience a breakdown of her identity.

This reached its peak during the middle of a two-week period in June following the sale of our home. Tom had to stay in the Bay Area to pack up all our belongings, put them into storage, finalize escrow paperwork, and take care of a number of details regarding the purchase of our new home, which wouldn't even be completed now until late July.

Tom spoke to Jayne over the phone on that Saturday night, when he'd normally have been with her and Nicholas. To hear his wife so unhappy, crying five hundred miles away, made him feel helpless at his end of the line. There was absolutely nothing he could do—except drop what he was doing, with the consequent loss of everything we'd worked toward since the day we were married.

Through it all, we both persevered, though there can be no doubt that for this stretch the burden lay squarely on Jayne. She did chores while Nicholas napped. She ran out quickly to empty the garbage or put in a load of laundry, always with an undercurrent of anxiety. While Jayne worried, Nicholas, of course, napped peacefully.

A clean environment is very important for a transplant patient. Daily Jayne vacuumed the small apartment and mopped the kitchen and bathroom floors. The bathtub also required disinfection each day before Nicholas took his bath.

In defining her needs to herself, Jayne realized that she needed some time alone—away from the pressures of full-time motherhood—yet she felt ambivalent about leaving Nicholas with another care-giver. Cheri came to her rescue, arranging for one of the nurses from the transplant unit to relieve Jayne one day for a few hours respite. Those brief hours were exhilarating: she browsed through a bookstore just blocks from the apartment and swam laps in the apartment pool, returning to the apartment relaxed and refreshed. Nicholas had slept the entire time.

More confident now about leaving him, Jayne interviewed students from the university and found a delightful young woman named Lana who knew infant CPR and was comfortable with the idea of caring for a heart transplant baby. Nicholas took to her fairly easily. At least now Jayne had some time for herself each week to run errands, grocery shop, and swim laps.

Tom's visits on the weekends were very special. Nicholas really missed his daddy. When Tom arrived at the nearby Ontario airport on Friday nights, Nicholas clapped with glee and wouldn't let Tom out of his sight. He wanted Daddy to hold him often and carry him if we went out for walks around the complex.

Because Nicholas could not be exposed to large groups of people, we could no longer worship as a family in a church community. Lana babysat on Saturday afternoons so that we could go to church and have an early dinner together.

We were aware that our lives were now so stretched that we were literally cramming a marriage into two or three short days each week. We missed each other. We missed our pleasant, quiet, happy family lifestyle, now left behind forever since our country log home had been sold. We cherished our time together each weekend, brief though it had to be. Those few hours alone together refreshed us. The memories of them sustained us during our lonesome times apart all week. We laughed and held hands across the table—and laughed some more. Our conversations, of course, always returned to Nicholas. Though we enjoyed our Saturday afternoon "dates," we missed our little brown-eyed boy.

Inevitably our outing would end with a stroll through the local mall and browsing in a bookstore, where we would buy Nicholas a book.

Nicholas was usually still awake at eight o'clock when we returned to the apartment. We'd read him a story from the new book and ready him for bed. As we sang him to sleep one Saturday evening, he reached out and touched both of us, one of his sweet little hands on Jayne's arm, the other on Tom's leg. The message was a strong one: *I like having both Mommy and Daddy with me.* He drifted off to sleep and we lay quietly in each other's arms. Clearly the stresses of the past few months and of being a "commuter" family had begun to drain us all. The stress recognized, we still had to go on as we were.

Dr. Bailey had said he'd consider allowing us to return home to the Bay Area four months after surgery if all continued to go well. That weekend we calculated that we had two and a half months yet to go. Those months felt like years as we looked ahead. Tom needed to protect his job; we simply couldn't survive without his income if we were going to have a home to return to in August. So we resolved to make the best of a difficult situation. In only ten weeks, our future would be bright again and our lives would return to semi-normalcy.

That Monday morning, we took Nicholas for his weekly checkup. Examined by the cardiologist, he had his regular X-ray, blood tests, EKG, and echocardiogram. As always, he remained cooperative for all procedures—except the blood tests. We stepped out of the room when the lab technician arrived, and Cheri stayed with Nicholas. As we stood in the hall, our hearts lurched with each of our son's screams. We'd learned the hard way that if either of us stayed in the room with him when he underwent painful procedures, he associated us not with the nurture and support that we thought we were giving him, but with the pain. We realized this soon after the time Jayne had stayed with Nicholas during the traumatic presurgery attempts to insert a feeding tube into his nose. For days afterward, he'd been suspicious of his mother. It had broken our hearts, and we had vowed never again to put ourselves in a similar position.

So now we had a new game. As soon as the lab tech pulled the needle out of Nicholas' arm, Cheri would call out, "All through now, Nicholas!" We'd hurry back into the room, and Jayne would throw her arms around him and say, "Mommy's here now, and I love you." The staff understood the reason for this "Sarah Bern-hardt" technique and went right along. Now that Mommy was the "rescuer," Nicholas calmed right down in her arms.

Though still showing signs of a mild rejection, all the test results that day showed that Nicholas was steadily improving. Medication was adjusted, and then we hurried to the airport. Nicholas slept in his car seat as Tom leaned over and kissed Jayne goodbye, then got out of the car and disappeared into the terminal. Nicholas didn't awaken until he and Jayne returned to the apartment complex and Jayne turned the car engine off. He opened his eyes, looked at Jayne, and smiled. He then looked around for Daddy, crying when he realized he was gone.

Jayne groaned. "It's going to be a very long ten weeks!"

⋖ई

The following Sunday, Nicholas' temperature and heart rate increased suddenly. We were told not to be alarmed, to bring him in the next morning for his regular eight o'clock Monday checkup. The next day proved unseasonably cool for Loma Linda. The weather in this Inland Empire region of southern California, forty miles west of Palm Springs, was typically quite warm and smoggy. We all wore sweaters that morning as we pushed Nicholas in his stroller through the hospital lobby. Invariably people looked, then looked again, at our little brown-eyed boy, who always wore a little yellow paper surgical mask over his mouth and nose when he visited the hospital.

The results of the tests that could be studied immediately were inconclusive, and the doctors said that they needed to see the results of all the tests before making a determination. But because of Nicholas' outwardly healthy appearance, they urged that Tom not cancel his plans to return to work.

Later in the day, just walking into the apartment after returning from the airport, Jayne answered the ringing phone. It was Cheri, calling to say that Nicholas showed signs of a "moderately severe" rejection and that Dr. Bailey wanted to admit him to the transplant unit. Jayne sighed and swung into action—packed some toys, books, and blankets, and a nightgown for herself, and bundled Nicholas up. An hour after Cheri's call, Nicholas was once again hospitalized.

Dr. Bailey had just returned from a three-week trip to Korea, where he had participated in a cardiac surgery teaching program. He greeted Jayne and Nicholas warmly, hugs all around, and they chatted about Nicholas' rejection episode.

"His heart is enlarged, and the voltage on his EKG is decreased," he began. "The cardiologist noted an extra heart sound this morning, which is also consistent with rejection. In addition, there's the pulse increase you and Tom observed over the weekend."

Jayne asked, "Do you think he ever got over the first mild rejection? Could this be a continuation of that one flaring up again now that he's off steroids?"

"Very likely that's exactly what's happening. I plan to begin a course of intravenous steroids tonight, and we'll keep a close eye on him. You should know that the increased steroids will make him moon-faced. He'll probably also get pretty fussy for a few days and be very hungry."

Nicholas reached out for Dr. Bailey, who was fast becoming an old buddy. Out the window of the room could be seen a helicopter landing on the hospital roof helipad. Dr. Bailey held Nicholas and told his little patient, "That's a chopper!" He made all sorts of noises to mimic the now quiet blades, and Nicholas giggled and grinned, pleased to have a daddy substitute around for a few minutes.

Jayne reached Tom by phone to alert him to the newest developments. "Darling, Nicholas is back in the hospital. Dr. Bailey doesn't seem to be worried, however. The only thing he plans is to start him on IV medications."

"Do you think I should fly right back down?" Tom asked.

"No, you should continue working and fly down on your regular Friday night flight. No one is particularly alarmed at this point."

"Do you promise to call me if there are any big changes?"

"Of course, but everything is really under control here. Nicholas is content, and I plan to spend the night in his hospital room."

"Okay, then, I'll stay up here and try to concentrate on work. I miss you both, and I love you."

"We love you too, darling. Night-night."

The following evening, Tom, who now lived at Katie's mother's home, returned from work and telephoned down to Loma Linda. He was put through to the nursing station on the transplant unit—only to be told by the clerk at the central desk that she couldn't put the call through to Nicholas' room.

"There's an awful lot of activity in there. I'd better not disturb them."

Instantly Tom became frightened. Clearly something was very wrong. "I *need* to speak to someone. I've got to know what's happening to my son. Is my wife there?"

"Hold on a moment, and I'll try to locate her."

Jayne wearily stood at a wall phone in the nurses' lounge, attempting to reach Tom and frustrated because the line was busy. The clerk poked her head in. "Mrs. Miller, your husband is calling. I'll transfer it in here."

Though in tears only moments before, Jayne tried to regain her composure. "Hi, Tommy."

"Jayne, what's happening? What's wrong with Nicholas?"

"Well, a few minutes before seven, he was asleep in my arms in the bedside rocking chair. I was talking to Sherrianne when suddenly he became limp and looked very pale. I glanced over at the cardiac monitor and his pulse rate, which had been in the 150s, was reading 45, then 30, then 20, then 15."

Jayne bit her lip, wanting to be brave. Enduring this when she was just down the hall from Nicholas was bad enough. For Tom, five hundred miles away, it would be much worse.

"The nurse called a doctor, who put a heart stimulant medicine in his IV, and his rate came right back up."

"What does Dr. Bailey say?"

"Dr. Bailey's in the O.R. doing a transplant on Baby Jesse. It's all over the news, radio, and TV down here. Things are very high stress. I've never seen so many reporters and TV cameras. The doctors in Nicholas' room are in communication with Dr. Bailey by phone, and as far as I can tell, Dr. Bailey's calling up orders for Nicholas even as he has his hands full with Jesse."

"Jayne, I'm going to fly back down tonight. I'll call the airlines right now. Stay by the phone, and I'll call you right back, okay?"

Tom ached with fear and desperation; He needed to be with his family! *There's an awful lot of activity in there* kept running through his mind over and over. He saw the worst. He had to get down there—NOW! He frantically flipped through the phone book and dialed an airline.

"Please book me on a flight to Ontario, California, tonight."

"I'm sorry, sir, our last flight left half an hour ago."

He tried another . . . and got put on hold. "Come on! Come on!" Trivialized pop tunes droned on and on in his ear.

Just then Katie walked in the door of her mother's house.

"Thank God you're here, Katie! I'm going out of my mind. I've never felt so helpless."

Hugging Tom, Katie said, "Jayne called and asked me to come stay with you. I'm so sorry. Is there anything I can do?"

"No. Just stay near."

"May I help you?" a telephone voice finally asked. Then, in response to Tom's request: "No, I'm sorry, all flights have already left this evening. But we have one to Los Angeles at midnight."

"No, thank you. That won't do."

In the end, no airline had flights available! What was he going to do? The Los Angeles airport was much too far away from Loma Linda. Finally he did all he *could* do: booked a seat on the earliest available flight in the morning—eight o'clock. Five hundred miles and thirteen hours separated him from his loved ones. He called

Jayne and explained that they had no choice; he'd arrive at the medical center in the morning.

Jayne hung up the phone and told Sherianne of Tom's plans. The social worker said she'd arrange to pick him up at the airport.

Just then, dressed in surgical scrubs, the chief of anesthesia came in to speak with Jayne and update her on Nicholas' condition. "I'm sure this must be frightening for you, Mrs. Miller. Your son experienced a severe symptom of rejection—something we call "heart block." The drop in his heart rate was caused by his heart's not conducting impulses as it normally would."

"How are you correcting this, Doctor?"

"As you know, Dr. Bailey has given medication orders, and Baby James appears stable now. Of course, his condition is quite serious and will require close monitoring. For the moment, however, we're encouraged."

"When can I go in to see him?"

"You can go in now for a few minutes. I'll check back with you later on tonight."

Jayne and Sherrianne gowned and masked and entered Nicholas' room. A doctor watched the cardiac monitor over the large crib, and two nurses made IV and equipment adjustments. Nicholas appeared pale and asleep. The monitor showed that his heart rate had returned to 153. Jayne sat quietly by the bed—feeling completely alone in her frustration, fear, and utter exhaustion.

At ten o'clock, Nicholas' heart rate plummeted again—this time only into the 70s. The team attending him was again galvanized into action. Sherrianne and Jayne went back to the nurses' lounge, and Jayne cried uncontrollably. Still standing, she leaned against the wood cabinets along the wall, pounded her fists against them, and screamed, "God! Please, after all this, please don't let my little boy die! Please God—NO!"

The next morning, Katie drove Tom to the airport, and by ten o'clock he had finally rejoined his wife and son. He hadn't slept the whole night; neither had Jayne. He held her tightly for a long moment. Then, after drinking in the sight of Jayne and their son, with Nicholas asleep in the crook of his mother's arm, apparently none the worse for wear, he heard about the sequel.

"Then, in the middle of the night," Jayne told him, "they took Nicholas to surgery for insertion of temporary pacemaker wires directly into his heart."

"You're sure they're temporary?"

"Yes. If his heart rate slows down again, this pacemaker"— Jayne held up a small box that had been in her lap—"will help get his heart back up to its regular rate. They brought him back here about four o'clock, and his heart rate has been stable ever since."

Jayne's words faded. She was so tired that it was difficult for her to talk. Tom, however, who'd been in the dark and in suspense for hours, needed answers desperately.

"Is there anything else?"

"Yes. Dr. Bailey started him on a very potent intravenous anti-rejection drug. He hasn't used it in any of his tiny patients before. But he says this rejection episode is clearly the worst they've seen yet in a child, so he felt it was indicated."

Tom pulled his chair up right next to Jayne's and held her hand. He sat with his loved ones near—and knew that as much as their lives had changed already, they were about to change still more—completely and irrevocably.

Once we were reunited, we both knew that there wasn't any way we could return to the Bay Area in the near future. For Nicholas' sake, we needed to stay near Loma Linda indefinitely. The new home that we'd dreamed so long about and had recently sacrificed so much for, would have to be let go.

Later that morning, Tom called the home builders and canceled. Now we had no home at all. Our belongings would remain in storage. Next Tom phoned his supervisor and arranged for an indefinite leave of absence.

Now that we'd all be living in southern California, our next order of business had to be finding larger quarters. Our one-bedroom furnished apartment was simply too small for the three of us.

One day the following week, while the nurses watched Nicholas, we responded to ads for rentals in the local classifieds. After looking at half a dozen nearby apartments and houses in our price range, we were disappointed to find nothing but dingy, unkempt properties. Moving into any one of them would have served only to drag our sinking spirits down even further.

The next day we saw an ad that captured our attention: "TOP OF THE WORLD. 4BR, 3BA townhouse in the trees. Furnished, pool, tennis! Must see! Call now."

Jayne told the person who answered the phone that Tom was a writer/editor. The gentleman became quite excited and spoke of the delights that his spacious townhouse in the mountains would hold for a writer and his family. He gave Jayne directions, and they made an appointment for the following weekend.

Meanwhile, in the confining hospital environment, Nicholas became increasingly fussy, suffering badly from boredom, lethargy, and general incomprehension of what was going on. Once again he required single-room isolation. Being a natural extrovert, he was perplexed by the ubiquitous yellow hospital gowns and blue masks that everyone wore and initially tried to pull them off. Though we provided him with exercise and visual stimulation, our creative efforts were limited by a small hospital room already filled with a crib and a bed. He wasn't allowed to sit on the floor to play, as we normally would have let him do at home, because the floor was the least sterile place in the room. There was simply no area—no normal playtime environment—that he could explore. He spent every minute *restricted* in his walker, on our laps, or in his crib. By nightfall of each day, we were exhausted and Nicholas was very unhappy. The gleeful glint in his eyes that had been so much a part of his happy personality was disappearing. His "lust for life" was ebbing. We felt frustrated, but what could we do?

Nicholas cried a lot—particularly if we left the room—and a screaming child is difficult to be patient with. Many of the nurses were approaching the limits of their tolerance. When we blamed the limitations of the solitary room and sterile procedure and explained that Nicholas was not being the pleasant little boy he typically was, some of them discounted our feelings as symptomatic of overanxious parents.

In fact, Nicholas was the first toddler transplanted at Loma Linda. Up to this point, the four other infants who'd had transplants there were newborns or infants of three months old or less. And many of the nurses were young and had no children of their own. For the most part, the transplant unit simply had no experience with the difficulties of the toddler age group, and many of the nurses failed to understand why Nicholas couldn't be as well behaved as their other transplant babies!

In an effort to lift Nicholas' spirits, we hung a twenty-five-foot Mylar rainbow kite around his room, canopying it overhead. We covered his walls with pastel Peanuts' character posters, and we mounted on the door a pint-sized basketball hoop that came with a small sponge ball. We romped the length of the room and back, and, for a time, we had Nicholas chasing us in his walker, watching for us to "sink a basket." He clapped with delight whenever we "made a point," as though he instinctively knew the object of the game. But his interest in this diversion didn't last long.

We also put on puppet shows for him, read stories, helped him color and draw pictures, blew bubbles, sang songs, played his new harmonica and baby piano, and encouraged him to play with various toys in his crib. We tried everything we could think of, but the facts of being stuck in that small room and being restricted in so many different ways won out. The last several days he spent there were horribly heart-breaking. The sparkle in our little boy's eyes had died, and nothing we tried seemed to make a difference. All he wanted to do was rest his head on our shoulders.

Realizing that there would be future cases similar to Nicholas', we suggested to the hospital that they develop a way to section off an area of a toddler's room and create a sterile—perhaps plastic—enclosed area complete with a small play structure and toys, to allow for autonomy and creative exploration. Soon we began to receive positive feedback from the transplant team and hospital staff. This was one of several times that we felt we were all learning together—pioneers, if you will—on the cutting edge of medical science and technology. In this instance, we had helped the hospital remember that the human spirit was important, too.

♪

Finally, after eleven days, we took Nicholas "home" again to the little furnished apartment. Three days after this, the Miller family excitedly embarked on a much-needed adventure. Up Waterman Avenue through San Bernardino and into the mountains, to look at the townhouse we'd seen advertised.

Our stay in the Inland Empire, as the area east of Los Angeles is called, was marked by the worst smog we'd ever experienced. Our eyes burned and we moaned daily, wondering how anyone could voluntarily live in such unpleasant conditions. Yet everywhere we turned, new homes were being built. The media filled air time and column space with predictions of rapid population growth into the next decade. We couldn't help but shake our heads at the paradox.

So to drive up into the San Bernardino Mountains and quickly rise above the smog and heat and see not only clear skies but bright flowering yellow Scotch broom and lush evergreen trees was truly a breath of fresh air. In fifteen minutes, we ascended five thousand feet. A little later, we approached the town of Blue Jay; then, continuing up the hill, we pulled into "Fernrock Estates," as the townhomes we'd come to see were colorfully called.

We introduced ourselves to the landlord. Nicholas, of course, enchanted the man, his wife, and the carpenter who was on hand helping get the place in shape for the new tenants.

Who we knew right away would be us.

Situated in the middle of an evergreen forest, on the edge of a mountain community, ten minutes from the glorious Lake Arrowhead resort and shopping complex, it seemed too good to be true.

The two-story, four-bedroom unit had a fireplace and a view of the hillside and trees from two balconies, and it was fully furnished besides. In addition, the rent was extremely modest. We liked the unit, the landlord liked us, and we made plans to move the following week, on June 30.

&

Life in Blue Jay quickly settled into a pleasant routine. Tom continued to work on his writing projects, spending time at his word processor each morning. We bought a toy typewriter for Nicholas, and our son banged happily on the keys, consciously emulating his daddy. Nicholas even had his own "office," a section of Daddy's table where he had within reach his new typewriter, a play telephone, and several of his favorite toys.

Jayne enjoyed swimming every day. As we pushed Nicholas along in his stroller toward the pool, he'd always check over his shoulder to be sure we were both there. When he made eye contact with each of us, he'd beam, then return his attention to the toy steering wheel and gear-shift lever mounted on his stroller.

Once in the water, Jayne did her laps, with her husband and son coaching her along. After she had exceeded the previous day's count, Tom brought Nicholas into the pool. Oh, Nicholas loved to swim! We'd hold him tightly and he'd splash and *splash*—and *laugh!* If we were sitting by the pool, we had to be alert to keep him from crawling right over the edge, he was so anxious to get back in! Naturally we started calling him "our Little Fish," in addition to his other nicknames of "Lamby Bear," "Sweety Lumps," "Sweet Pea," and "Little Guy."

The clean, airy environment of Blue Jay was good for everybody. No sooner had we settled in than our son entered another period of great developmental progress.

We usually gave him his medicines and took his vital signs while he lay on the living room couch. He loved playing with the stethoscope as we listened to his heart; our challenge each time was to find some other object that would hold his attention long enough so that we could count his heartbeats. When we were done, if he didn't hop off, he'd strut around on the cushions holding onto the back of the couch. One day while doing this, he discovered the light switch, which was right within arms' reach above the couch. The first time he flicked the switch in late afternoon and all the lights went on in the living room, you would have thought that he was Sir Isaac Newton being hit on the head with an apple. He looked at his dad with a great, *Did I do that?* look of wonder. Then he flicked the switch in the other direction. Now this was magic! Thereafter, he became a great student of "cause and effect as pertaining to light switches."

He also discovered sliding doors. Regular hinged doors had previously been his number 1 joy, but now he'd stand for a half-hour at a time by any one of the four sliding screen doors that led out to the child-proofed balconies and open and close, open and close, clearly astonished by this new mechanism.

Months before, Nicholas had been given a toy that made farmyard animal sounds if a string was pulled. Though he enjoyed the sounds it made, he was oblivious to the string. Then one day, as Tom was holding the toy, Nicholas came right up to it and yanked on the string just as though he'd been practicing. This time it was Dad's turn to be astonished!

One night about this same time, we tried to put Nicholas to sleep in his crib just as we had done every night for most of his life; *this* night he pitched a fit and screamed at the top of his lungs. We weren't exactly clear what the problem was, but because we always tried to treat Nicholas as normally as possible, we did what every child-care book and experienced parent had suggested to us. We let him cry, with periods of hugging. We were determined not to let him get his way—whatever that was! This went on for three nights. Our poor neighbors must have been at the end of their rope. Then we had the idea that maybe it was time for Nicholas to switch to a twin bed. We tried it, and—*voilà!* One happy child again!

Two weeks after this, Nicholas took full advantage of his new-found freedom. One afternoon he awakened from his nap, climbed out of bed, and crawled quietly into the adjacent hallway, past the room where his mother sat reading, and up two flights of stairs. He announced himself with a yelp of glee as he entered Tom's office. Tom jumped—and called Jayne. Hearing her son mysteriously upstairs, Jayne raced to see. Sure enough, Nicholas had climbed the stairs for the first time all by himself, yet he'd never showed even a passing interest in them before. Now that he had mastered the trick of climbing, there would be no stopping him; he had taken still another step toward independence.

᪄

Each week we spent one day down in the Loma Linda area, for Nicholas' early-morning doctor visit, errands, and visits with our new friends. We'd developed special friendships with some of the nurses and their families and with other hospital staff members. We'd met still other friends through our church. We felt very blessed—lucky even—to have adjusted fairly readily to what only three months before had been completely unknown territory to us.

And yet, despite all our good fortune during this complex and stressful time, a complication arose that we hadn't expected. Never in our married lives had we spent so much time together. At first being together as a family during this period of crisis seemed the answer to all our prayers, but very slowly—not even realizing it at first—we began to get on each other's nerves.

By the beginning of August, it seemed that the least little thing suddenly became a cause for bickering. Tom snapped at Jayne for staying on the phone too long. Jayne snapped at Tom for using too much soap in the laundry. And on and on. Misunderstandings turned into quarrels, quarrels into full-blown arguments. It wasn't because we didn't love one another; it was because of fear, exhaustion, uncertainty about so many things, too much close proximity, the feeling of being uprooted, that constant undercurrent of anxiety, and the nagging sensation that our whole life had been transplanted. The stress of our entire difficult situation had come to a head.

Suddenly we found ourselves fearing for ourselves—on top of all our fears for Nicholas. Could we survive as a couple? Would our *family* make it?

What must Nicholas have felt or thought in his own way during this period? Lord knows we tried to insulate him from it.

◆§

In mid August, Jayne turned thirty-two years old, and her parents flew down to celebrate the event. Nicholas was truly delighted to see his grandparents again—particularly Grandpa, who tickled him and played peekaboo. We had a wonderful and relaxing three-day visit. Nicholas' eyes grew round as he watched his mommy blow out the candles on her chocolate cake. He clapped his hands as we all sang "Happy Birthday." No doubt he thought we were singing for him, because we always sang "Happy Birthday" to him on the fifteenth of each month. But candles—this was new and fascinating!

Katie had sent Nicholas an inflatable boat in the package with Jayne's birthday present. We inflated it and took it into the pool with us that day. Grandma pushed the boat with Nicholas in it. He laughed as he looked over the edge at the water below. The temperature reached eighty-five degrees that afternoon, and we all enjoyed playing in the water.

We were sad to say goodbye to Jayne's parents. For several days following their departure, we'd ask Nicholas, "Where's Grandpa?" and he'd crawl quickly over to the guest room. Then we'd either phone to let him hear Grandpa's voice or show him Grandma and Grandpa's picture. He also visibly brightened whenever he heard Tom's mother's voice on the phone. Clearly he remembered and recognized her voice. Again we'd reinforce the connection with pictures.

By this time, we better understood what was happening to

us—why we were frequently not happy when we should have been. We learned to recognize the symptoms of irritability as they began to appear. We even had a name for our irritability: we called it the Submarine Syndrome. Being cooped up in our new home high in the mountains, far away from our real home, with more pressure to deal with than many people ever dream of . . . all this contributed to the Submarine Syndrome, and once we recognized it and labeled it, we learned to nip the symptoms in the bud and the joy began to return to our lives.

August 18, a red-letter day! All of Nicholas' test results at that week's regular checkup were completely normal. We were told, "If you didn't know he had a heart transplant, you wouldn't be able to tell it from the test results." We were elated; everything was coming along just fine! His course of steroid medication had even been completed, and his puffiness had gone away.

But so had his appetite. The steroids had caused him to be unusually hungry, and now that he was off them, it was difficult to get him to eat anything at all. Except for whatever was in his bottle, food had lost its allure. The doctors had explained that this would happen, so we weren't too concerned. Besides, one way or another, we were able to cajole or sneak food into him.

The following Tuesday, August 26, the medical report was equally encouraging—so much so that the cardiologist scheduled our next appointment for *two* weeks later. Nicholas was no longer going to be seen weekly. On the way out, we saw Bill Hinton, the chaplain who had been so kind to us the day of Nicholas' surgery. We shared with him the good news of Nicholas' continued progress. As we chatted, Jayne suddenly remembered that this day was the four-month anniversary of Nicholas' transplant. Somehow it seemed so much longer than four months. . . .

A few days later, having heard from friends that there was an extraordinary indoor shopping mall called South Coast Plaza "only two hours" away, we decided to hop in the car and have an adventure. It was a warm day—*hot* is actually the word—but we toughed it out and arrived at our destination. And it was worth the long drive. To see again row after row of exotic shops and boutiques was a great change of pace for us all. Naturally we spent a lot of time in the bookstores, but the *pièce de résistance* was the merry-go-round!

At the corner where two rows of shops came together, there was a small but functioning merry-go-round with about twenty horses. Without a second's hesitation, we decided that Nicholas would take his first merry-go-round ride. Jayne boarded and sat Nicholas on one of the outside horses, carefully strapping him on. As the calliope played and the ride began turning, Nicholas got a *very* concerned look on his face, especially when he realized that Daddy was standing off to one side and fast getting out of sight. But in a moment, the ride had gone full circle, and *there* was Daddy. Around and around. It took three or four revolutions, but our son finally got the idea that this was *FUN!* When this struck home, his frown became a smile, and his smile grew broader and broader. He was just full of grins when it stopped and he and Mommy rejoined his proud dad.

Friday, while Jayne chatted with a friend on the telephone, Nicholas played happily near his toybox. Books and blocks were strewn about the living room floor. With no warning, he vomited. We immediately rechecked his pulse rate and temperature, which had been fine earlier, and all still appeared normal. Noting the incident on his daily medication report, we presumed that this was an isolated incident. (There had been other, similar incidents of vomiting associated with his being weaned off of steroids.) The afternoon and evening passed uneventfully.

Saturday morning we were up early; we had chores to do and errands to run. Tom needed to go out and buy a used washing machine, but that afternoon we planned to take Nicholas to Santa's Village, a local tourist attraction complete with an ice-covered North Pole outside Santa's workshop. Nicholas, though, had no appetite for breakfast and appeared somewhat listless. After being given his morning medications, he even refused his bottle—but otherwise he seemed happy enough. At eleven-thirty he vomited again, and Jayne became alarmed. She phoned Cheri, who conferred with the pediatrician on call for the transplant service, then advised us to bring Nicholas into the emergency room to be seen—just to be on the safe side.

As soon as Tom returned home from his errand, Jayne updated him and off we went to Loma Linda. Nicholas was wearing a pinstriped sailor suit and his navy-blue leather sandals, and the emergency room staff nurses all cooed over him and told us how cute he looked. He sat grinning on the E.R. gurney, as if to say, "I know that I'm the center of attention." His energy was back; he surely didn't appear ill. We started to think we'd come all the way down the mountain for nothing.

But when the pediatric resident examined him, he heard an abnormal heart sound. He ordered tests, and off we went once again for an EKG and the rest of the gamut. It was decided that Nicholas should be admitted for observation, and since it would take an hour for a bed to be made available on the transplant unit, we decided to go out for a quick dinner. Nicholas still had no appetite, refusing even a graham cracker, but he seemed cheerful and energetic, giggling and waving at a woman sitting at a nearby table.

We were depressed at the thought of Nicholas having to be readmitted. Our conversation centered around how we could make this hospitalization less stressful and difficult for him than the last. As parents, we felt frustrated that our young son would again be subjected to hospital isolation and abnormal routines. The reality of the *chronic* nature of Nicholas' condition really began to hit us.

When we returned to the hospital, Nicholas' room was ready. We had just gotten settled into it when Dr. Bailey strode in to examine his brown-eyed, active patient. Tom and Nicholas showed the doctor how well our son could walk, holding on to only one paternal fingertip. Then Nicholas spied a cupboard in the corner of the room and went right over to open it. As he moved the door to and fro, examining the hinges, Dr. Bailey remarked how well he looked; he said that the lab work and vital signs so far appeared quite acceptable as well. We were quite relieved to hear this!

"I think we should admit him for observation overnight, since he's here. Just to be sure," he said with a wink and a grin.

"If all of the other tests come back normal, we'll let you all go home in the morning. In the meantime, I'll have the nurses set up a cot and a recliner chair in here so that you can stay the night with Nicholas."

Nicholas had been sleeping in a "big-boy bed" for nearly six weeks now at home, so we were unsure how he'd react to being placed in the hospital crib. But ever the adventurer, he explored it and the adjacent wall meters and valves happily and never so much as whimpered. *Gee, look at all these neat things on the walls. Oh, they look like fun,* he seemed to think.

Moments later, Dr. Bailey reentered the room.

"I have some bad news, folks. The chest X-ray shows that Nicholas' heart is quite enlarged, and his EKG voltage is decreased. The echocardiogram is also abnormal. Along with the abnormal heart sound, it appears that this little boy is trying to reject his new heart again."

"But his vitals were all normal—not anything like the last time he rejected. And the lab work is also normal," Jayne protested.

"It's mysterious; I'll grant you that. We've never seen this before, and I don't understand it myself. But it's clear that he *is* rejecting, and our best course is to start immediate IV steroid therapy. We'll also adjust his cyclosporine dosage."

The doctor needed to begin procedures, so we hugged our little guy and stepped out of the room until the IV was successfully in place. When we went back in, Nicholas was hooked up to an overhead IV bottle and also to the heart monitor. And he was *very* unhappy. When Tom tried to give him his nightly medications, Nicholas vomited them immediately. Tom picked up his son and held him tightly, and they both cozied up in the recliner as Jayne lay down on the cot and covered herself up. As Tom sang "Silent Night" quietly, Nicholas put his head on his daddy's shoulder.

Jayne said, "Goodnight, Tommy. I'm grateful to God for you and for Nicholas."

"Goodnight, darling. I'm also grateful to God for you and Nicholas."

It was the last thing we said to one another every night before we dropped off to sleep. Tom brushed a curl from his son's forehead and said, "God protect you, my son. I love you." Without fail, it was the last thing he said to Nicholas each night when he put his son to sleep.

Just as he had in the wee hours before surgery, Tom held Nicholas on his shoulder all night as Jayne slept fitfully.

At five-thirty Jayne awoke and took Nicholas into her cot. He dozed but was clearly uncomfortable with the IV and chest leads. A little later, he guzzled a bottle right down. We were encouraged by this.

At seven, though, Nicholas began dry-heaving, and a moment later his color turned pale and gray. The doctor who came in to investigate thought that the change in color was due to muscular contraction associated with retching. He ordered oxygen, and immediately Nicholas' color perked up and he seemed happier, although he wasn't pleased about having the oxygen tube taped under his nose and kept trying to pull it off.

At eleven Nicholas turned pale again. Knowing how important the oxygen was, Tom was struggling to keep the tube in place when Dr. Bailey, who'd been called in from home, entered to examine Nicholas. The doctor surveyed the scene and led us from the room, then called in a team of nurses and doctors who swung into action. As we left that room, the last sight of our son was of him frowning.

Though we were tremendously concerned, this incident didn't seem any worse than the many other crises we had shared with

Nicholas. When we left that room, we were confident that the doctors would reverse whatever was happening and that our son would bounce back—*just as he always did!*

Sherrianne took us to a nearby empty office and awaited events with us.

Half an hour later, Tom, who was restlessly wandering through the unit, peeked through a window into Nicholas' room. Dr. Bailey saw him and came out to say that he had needed to sedate Nicholas so that our little boy wouldn't be uncomfortable. The doctor had also inserted a breathing tube and attached Nicholas to a respirator. He went on to explain that Nicholas' heart was beating very irregularly and that he'd begun administering the same potent antirejection drug that had helped pull Nicholas through his last rejection.

He put his hand on Tom's shoulder and said, "You know, Tom, whatever happens in this room today, whatever may happen with Nicholas, you must always remember that you and Jayne exist on a plane different from the life you have with Nicholas. The love that you and Jayne have for one another must always stand by itself. Do you understand?"

"Yes, I understand."

"You must always love Nicholas, of course, but you and Jayne must come first. I don't know what's going to happen today, but you have to understand what I'm saying."

Tom nodded, nearly dumbstruck by the implications, and went back to report to Jayne.

At one o'clock, Tom got up again to check on his son. This time the blinds were closed in the door window, but he could see clearly enough through the cracks. The little room was crowded with half a dozen people. He couldn't see Nicholas because a doctor stood blocking the view. As Tom watched, however, the doctor moved, and Tom could see that Dr. Bailey was doing CPR on his little boy.

CPR. Cardiopulmonary resuscitation. The last-ditch effort to save a life. His son was dying; he saw it with his own eyes.

But no! Remember, back at Stanford: the night Nicholas fibrillated they did CPR on him for fifteen minutes, and he survived. No, things weren't hopeless yet.

In a state of shock, he went back to the office where Jayne and Sherrianne waited. "They're doing CPR," he said. There was nothing else to say.

Jayne only stared. Minutes became eternities. We both cried.

Half an hour later, we both went to check. There was less activity. Dr. Bailey spotted us and came out.

"Nicholas is in critical condition. We had to do CPR on him for nearly twenty minutes. He has a rhythm now, and we're treating him vigorously. We still hope to get ahead of this massive rejection. But I've had Cheri register him with the Regional Organ Procurement Association. We may have to consider doing another transplant." He shrugged. "The chances of a donor organ becoming available are slim."

Tom was looking intently into the room. "Can we go in now, Doctor?"

"Why don't you wait about fifteen minutes? We'll come and get you." And then he went back into Nicholas' room.

Fifteen minutes came and went. After a time, Sherrianne said, "I'll go and check."

She came back pale and obviously nervous. Jayne took one look at the social worker and felt a rush of adrenalin course through her body.

"I'm afraid they're doing CPR again."

Tom slumped over the desk and cried. "Please, God, let the miracle of that little boy continue. Please don't let it end. We love him so. Please."

Jayne stared quietly ahead, too numb to cry.

The minutes turned to hours. The CPR continued.

No string of words can ever describe the anguish we experienced. What are words next to the infinite sense of loss? Our every thought was a prayer, and every prayer was an agonized plea for yet another miracle in the life of this precious, incredible little boy who had always somehow bucked the odds.

We wept alone. We wept in each other's arms. We wept in the hallway and in front of Nicholas' room. All the while clinging to the hope that our son would make it . . . but fearing all the while that we had run out of miracles.

There came a point when Tom, realizing that the end was near, needed to be with his son more than anything else in the world. But he was blocked from entering the room—blocked by nothing more than a door and hospital protocol. It's strange, but even in this most stressful situation, civilized behavior predominated. One would think he would've simply barged in, but part of his mind knew that such behavior would accomplish nothing. He agonized. How could he get inside that room?

On one of his pilgrimages back and forth from the office to Nicholas' room, he found Dr. Bailey on the phone at the nursing station. Seizing his chance, he scribbled a note on a piece of paper and handed it to the doctor. It read, "Doctor, I *must* be with my son." Dr. Bailey read the note and squinted at Tom as he spoke on the phone. Tom returned to Jayne and Sherrianne.

Fifteen minutes later, at a quarter to eight, we were both in front of Nicholas' room when Dr. Bailey stepped out. "Let's talk," he said and led us back to the office.

"The rejection has completely overwhelmed the heart. None of the treatments that worked before has any effect now. The heart muscle is simply incapable of beating on its own. For now we're continuing CPR, but we've done just about all we can do."

"Are there no options, Doctor?" Tom asked.

"All we could do is try putting him on the heart-lung machine— but we know from recent experience that cerebral damage is likely. We could try it, but I can't guarantee anything. In the end, Nicholas in all probability wouldn't be Nicholas any longer."

"So we really have no choice."

"I'm afraid not."

"Doctor, we must be allowed to be with him."

"Under normal conditions, Tom, that wouldn't be allowed. But because of your backgrounds, I'm going to make an exception.

We'll continue working on him for another hour. Beyond that, if we haven't seen some improvement or received a donor call . . ." He let the words hang.

We held hands and followed Dr. Bailey to our son's room.

Nicholas was sedated and unresponsive, and a breathing tube was in place. Three nurses, two doctors, and a respiratory therapist all worked feverishly, continuing CPR, adjusting IVs, and checking monitors.

Tom went to one side of the bed while Jayne went to the other. We stroked his dark curls and whispered encouraging words into his ear. We alternated talking to our unconscious little boy. Memories of our encouraging litanies from Stanford eighteen months before flooded back.

"We love you, Nicholas, and we want you."

"Life's an adventure, little guy, and we'll have lots of fun exploring together."

"Nick-Nick-Nick-Nick-Nicholas—we love a little boy named Nicholas."

"Let your heart beat strong and steady, little guy . . . strong and steady."

"Ah . . . ah . . . ah . . . *choo!*"

"Kipling can't wait to see you again. He hasn't seen you in *so* long."

After forty minutes, Jayne looked down at her little boy and knew he was dying. She'd seen death many times before in her work at the hospital; she'd learned to recognize it.

"Nicholas," she said, "we had you baptized so that you could have the gift of eternal life. I love you, Lamby Bear, and I'll miss you always. Please look down on Mommy and Daddy from up in Heaven and protect us, okay?" Her tears splashed on the crib sheets. She looked up at her loving husband. "Darling," she asked, "have you ever seen anyone die before?"

He shook his head, unable to speak through his sobs.

"Let's step into the corner. I need to share with you what it may be like."

Moments later Dr. Bailey joined us. His shoulders were drooping, the gleam gone from his eyes. "I really think we've done all that we can. You can decide when you want us to stop. I'm so sorry."

"Doctor?" Jayne asked. "Would it be possible to get some warm blankets to wrap Nicholas in?"

As the doctor quietly passed on the request to one of the nurses, we approached the bed and whispered our farewells to this very special boy whom we had been privileged to parent.

The warm blankets arrived. Nicholas was wrapped in them by Dr. Bailey and Cheri. They looked at us and we nodded together. Dr. Bailey touched the shoulder of the doctor who'd been doing chest compressions all this time, and the man stopped.

Seconds later, at 8:58 P.M., as we quietly wept, his father clasping his little boy's hands, Nicholas Lawrence Miller died in his mother's arms, his small form now still forever.

THE CONCLUSION

With more pain in our beings than is comprehensible, we said our final goodbye to Nicholas. We stroked his curly brown hair one last time, studied his delicate hands and feet, gently touched his flawless face, and kissed his long eyelashes. We took in all we could—and then were faced with the fact of having to leave that room. Having made sure that he was bundled snugly in the blanket, we somehow passed, with some gentle coaxing from Cheri, into the nursing station beyond, and the door closed behind us. Someone placed some papers in front of us, and we signed them— consents and releases and so on.

Understanding that we couldn't drive up the mountain alone on that terrible, shroud-black night, Cheri insisted that we stay at her house. We moved as if sleepwalking. People spoke to us, offering their sympathy. We thanked them. But it was like being in a play. None of this could *really* be happening.

The quiet ride to the Mathis home seemed interminable, though it lasted less than twenty minutes. Jayne thought, *I know the night has never seemed this dark to me.* We held hands in the back seat. The simplest movement or action required concentration: *Let's see, I should open the car door and step out. . . .*

The tears that night were unending; they flowed openly. Consciousness ached, and we longed for the oblivion of sleep. We both swallowed sleeping pills. Tom left a lamp on in the room, a practice he continued for several more weeks.

In the morning, consciousness returned. For months this first morning moment, whether eyes were opened or closed, would be the worst. With consciousness came realization. Came reality. Came pain. We thought of Nicholas in Heaven. Why were we thrust so totally into Hell?

People surrounded us, cushioning us. Our Loma Linda friends visited, sipped refreshments with us in Cheri's living room. People were genuinely sorry. They gave of themselves.

Katie flew down immediately. We'd been awake only a few hours when she swept into Cheri's house. Katie—our ever-present support and consolation. Her wise words struck an immediate chord: "If the doctors had told you when Nicholas was born that they could make him well, but only for eighteen and a half months, you know you still would have chosen him." With this poignant—and true—perspective in our hearts and minds, we were able to sit down calmly and write our contribution to the press release that the Medical Center would distribute to announce Nicholas' death. We'd preserved our anonymity thus far mainly to protect Nicholas. Now that there was no longer a need, we allowed the hospital to release all of our names. In hours the world would learn the truth, such as it was, about Baby James.

We were grateful beyond measure to have been this boy's parents—and *yes, if we had known then, at his birth, what we know now, we still would have wanted him, loved him, and been grateful for every minute we shared with him.*

Katie drove us home to Blue Jay, where we were confronted with the shock and sadness of Nicholas' not being there. Every corner, every piece of furniture had memories attached. This was the last home we would know together. We cried so much.

The phone rang constantly—supportive friends and family from all over the country offering their condolences—even some from as far away as Germany, where our loss had been reported in the military newspaper, *The Stars and Stripes.* We felt lucky that so many people cared.

Our "shadow selves" emerged. Jayne—the extrovert—became quiet and passive, while Tom—the introvert—handled the deluge of phone calls. He had to keep occupied; Jayne needed to be quiet with her thoughts. Through it all, Katie remained close by.

Jayne's mother helped us plan Nicholas' memorial service, which was to be held at the church where we had worshiped as a family before our sudden relocation to southern California. We wanted it to be very personal—*a celebration of life.*

When Fr. Miles phoned, shaken, Jayne reminisced about the wonder Nicholas had shown in clapping. "We want people to clap, Miles—for Nicholas and for the great joy he gave to so many. And laughter: don't be afraid to encourage those present to laugh as Nicholas did—often and with great delight. And the music: it will be all of Nicholas' favorites."

Three days later, four priests gathered at the altar to concelebrate. There were many people in the church, so many of whom Nicholas had inspired with his own courage. We greeted each at the door. *What force is propping us up?* we mused.

Fr. Miles' tears flowed as he recalled for the crowd Nicholas' christening and first birthday in that very church little more than six months before. "It's okay to cry today for the one whom we have lost, a very special and brave little boy."

On a table in front of the altar was a framed enlargement of a photo of a gleeful Nicholas—taken five days before he died. And surrounding the photo was a collection of "special things" that we had chosen to share with the assembly: Nicholas' first rattle, his plastic Kermit, his stuffed Mickey Mouse, his toy typewriter, several of his books, his jack-in-the-box (symbolizing his fascination with hinges), his last sailor suit, the sandals he had worn nearly every day in southern California, his bottle of bubbles, and a wall plaque that had been a gift from a friend—a handmade wooden heart that bore the Scripture quote "I will give you a new heart and place a right spirit within you."

When Jayne had first brought up with Miles the idea of sharing these mementos, he'd suggested, "Why don't you also ask close family and friends to stand and speak of the significance of each item?"

The night before the service, when we were trying to decide whom we should ask, Tom looked at Jayne and said, "There are only two people who can do this right."

"Yes?"

"You and I."

"Tommy, I really don't think I'm strong enough."

"You and I were his parents. Only we can talk about his things."

Gaining strength in her heart from Tom's own resolve, Jayne agreed, requesting only that he speak first.

When the time came, we both stood and took turns explaining each item in chronological order. Out flowed the story of our little boy.

During the eulogy that followed, Fr. Miles fought to keep his voice from breaking. Among his kind words was this remembrance: "Just after Nicholas died, I spoke to Jayne and Tom. Two of the things that they said stuck in my mind. Tom said, 'I have to believe that God wanted Nicholas to learn something, and that we were chosen to be his teachers; then, when our little boy had learned it, he was called back to the Father. It's the only thing that makes sense.' And Jayne—she put it so simply: 'How can we begrudge our little boy eternal life?' Indeed, how can we?"

Then Miles invited everyone in the congregation to share their own prayers and special memories. Many of those gathered spoke their prayers for us, spoke of their gratitude at having known our young son. All the while, Nicholas' smiling face beamed before the assembly, reminding us of the joy he had known—a joy that was now complete.

Afterwards many expressed to us how deeply they were moved by the completeness of the liturgy—the songs and stories, the clapping and singing, the sadness and joy. For weeks people reflected with us, saying repeatedly, "It was the happiest funeral I've ever attended."

The last song sung that day was "Silent Night." It's final lines were also our most fervent prayer for our son: "Sleep in heavenly peace, Sleep in heavenly peace."

~§

Five weeks later, we returned to the Bay Area, rented an apartment, and returned to our jobs. During this period, our grief was a pain without end. As never before, we needed to be each other's best friend.

The shock that insulated us during that first week at home wore off quickly. Before long, friends and family went back to living life as usual. We were left alone with our great loss. We clung to one another for strength. Often we would wake in the middle of the night crying.

Jayne told Tom: "I feel as if I've been ripped open, hollowed out, by someone's fingernails scratching deep into my exposed flesh. My pain is blinding and violent."

Tom often felt as if he were drowning in his sorrow, sometimes literally having to gasp for air. His knees were weak, making it difficult to stand. This confusing instability usually gave way to nausea.

It bears repeating: sleep was the one relief from our wakeful pain and sorrow. But awakening only intensified our feelings of loss. Often during the first seconds after awakening, we would listen for Nicholas as we had been so used to doing—only to remember a moment later that he had died.

Jayne dreamed often and consolingly of Nicholas. He was as she imagined him—smiling, dressed in a white garment, wearing a garland of laurel leaves in his curly hair. Once he was with a favorite aunt and a friend who had died. Jayne awoke feeling he was okay and being mothered.

Tom cried out incessantly, "It wasn't supposed to happen this way! How can I be the guiding star of his existence now?" In the beginning, the memories hurt so much that he prayed to be able to forget. Later he found himself forgetting little moments and prayed to be able to remember every precious detail.

Disorientation became the norm. Life became a matter of going through the motions, of putting one foot in front of the other. This was the only way we could make it: *one foot in front of the other.*

We thought of Nicholas' birthparents often. Did they know? Had they heard about "Baby James" at any time? Had they seen our names in the final reports? We wondered if they'd want to know.

~§

Included in the outpouring of sympathy were many books on grief. We found comfort in these but were dismayed by a much-repeated statistic: 90 percent of parents who lose a child through death are divorced within the first year. Chaplains, social workers, counselors, doctors, and nurses confirmed this distressingly high number.

We didn't want to become part of this statistic, and we consciously affirmed this to one another. A thought had come to Jayne one day: *If I should lose Tom, I would lose the one person who truly knew the depth of our experience with Nicholas.* She shared this with Tom, and together we allowed this thought to become the bedrock of our future life together.

We recalled the night that Tom had proposed marriage so many years before. Was it really eight years already? He'd taken Jayne in his arms and looked down into her eyes, asking, "Will you be the mother of my children? Will you love me all the days of our lives? Will you help me to build a granite foundation that will be the solid base for the sculpture of our life together?" Jayne felt her spine tingle as she savored that precious memory.

The strength of that foundation has carried us through much— has resisted the shattering power of the inevitable questions: Why him? Why us? The sculpture is intact; the foundation has held.

We spent our time together. We learned quickly the meaning of honoring each other's grief. Encouraging the free expression of tears kept us close, as did laughter while remembering happy moments with Nicholas.

As we wrote down our story, we often became lost in the reality of those moments, and then, as if we'd been slapped in the face, we'd realize that Nicholas' life had been torn away from us, that it had been reduced to just two dimensions—a photo, a sheet of paper. New questions surfaced: Will the pain ever end? Will the grief ever go away? Often we longed for just one more day, even one more hour, with our little boy.

New perspectives came, rationalizations of our loss. "How lucky we were to have known such quality in another person." "If we had to lose him, weren't we lucky that it was while he was still an innocent?" "At least our memories aren't marred by guilt." "We have only happy memories."

In both life and death, Nicholas pushed the threshold of medical knowledge forward a bit. His doctors looked constantly for new answers. We've learned from some of these doctors that the knowledge they gained while treating our son has directly benefited other children. We've been told, also, that at least two babies are alive today because of knowledge gleaned from Nicholas' death. We've sought solace in this . . . to little avail.

There are so many whys. "Why did he survive initially?" "If God gave him the gift of a miracle, why was his time so short?" "Why had he been given the gift of a successful transplant only to die four months later?" "Why had he checked out perfectly only a week before?" "Why didn't his heartrate or his temperature increase as they *should have* during a rejection?" WHY? There were so many questions. As they surfaced, we held one another, patiently seeking to help the other.

We didn't hesitate to seek counseling or join grief support groups. Each helped in its own way and offered us coping skills. The knowledge that others had survived similar losses gave us hope that we would also. One such group, called The Compassionate Friends, works specifically with parents who have lost children.

•⋖ʃ

Because we're two different people, we mourn differently and at different rates. It is largely due to this universal difference that couples move away from one another—first emotionally, then physically, then permanently. Generally one starts feeling stronger sooner than the other and fails to understand why the other "persists in wallowing in tears." The "stronger" partner then loses patience. The emotional conflict snowballs, with divorce the final result.

Patience is imperative. It is an important part of *honoring one another's grief.* Our wedding vows, said seven years before our tragedy, took on a meaning we had never anticipated: "I will love you and honor you all the days of my life."

Honoring each other's grief—the tears, the sadness, the pain we could see in the other's eyes. We grieved intensely and together. We spoke freely of our pain and denied each other no avenue of expression.

Often parents who have lost a child decide together, or by way of an edict issued by one or the other, that "there will be no more mention of *him* or *her* in this house." This well-intentioned approach places a "grief void" in the family. The pain continues and grows, but remains unspoken. This is one pitfall we fortunately avoided.

For months after Nicholas died, Tom was unable to bear looking at our son's many pictures. But Jayne needed to retreat to them each day. Tom put away the many framed pictures around the house, those reminders of his son like knives to his heart. Jayne honored Tom's need while privately seeking to honor her own; she looked at pictures during private moments and remembered.

In December Jayne broached the subject of pictures once again, but Tom still felt unready to have them hanging in our apartment. By week's end, however, Tom had placed a small framed snapshot of Nicholas sitting in the tulip garden of our country home on her desk.

"He's about nine months old in that picture," he said. "In many ways he was still a baby then. I simply can't handle anything more recent."

Jayne was delighted to have this picture on the desk where she spent so much of her time each day. How dear of Tom to honor her need by placing it there. We had both learned lessons of patience with our own and each other's needs.

Christmas would have been a difficult time if we hadn't anticipated the pain and made special plans. How much different it would have been if Nicholas had been with us! We chose not to celebrate with our families that year. Instead, we spent a quiet holiday away from all but each other. A quaint hotel in a foggy city housed our subdued celebration of the Lord's birth. Our hope was that Nicholas was in the midst of great joy.

We found that grief added a new depth and dimension to our relationship. We were committed to not allowing it destroy us, and, in that struggle, found that it brought us still closer together. We wanted to parent again.

Early on we became aware of how very much we missed being parents. We had lost our only child *and* we had lost our identity as parents. Never before had either of us begun to appreciate the identity crisis death could bring. Losing a spouse leaves the survivor no longer a husband or wife. When children lose their parents, they are no longer sons or daughters. We grieved the loss of parenthood while grieving the loss of our precious child. Our little boy was only a memory.

To this day, we wince when asked if we have children—should we tell them about Nicholas? Sometimes we do; more often we just utter a quiet "no"—a cruel reminder that we are no longer parents. We have, however, committed to creating our family anew through adoption. It is our fervent hope that someday a birthmother will choose us to become the parents of her child.

During the months that followed our loss, Tom often thought back to his feeling that our son had come to earth to learn something. He pondered this over and over, reasoning through it. *If so, what could he possibly have learned? If Jayne and I were his teachers, what did we teach him?*

One day he said to Jayne, "If Nicholas came face to face with God, and God asked, 'Well, Nicholas, what did you learn down there?' what do you think would be his answer?"

Jayne thought about this and said, "I think he'd answer, 'I learned that Mommy and Daddy wanted me and loved me very much.'"

"Yes," said Tom, "that's so true, but there's got to be more. What else did we instill in that little boy during his eighteen and a half months?"

Jayne responded, "Well, we tried to make an adventure out of every little thing we did—whether going grocery shopping or playing in the garden or going out to dinner."

"That's it; that's what I'm getting at. I think he'd say to God, 'I learned that my Mommy and Daddy wanted and loved me very much *and that life is an adventure.*'"

Jayne nodded thoughtfully. "Yes, I believe that. I really believe that's true."

❦

Whatever else we might seek or learn in our attempts to make sense of it all—of the miracle and of the miracle's end—we truly believe that Nicholas was a gift to us, and that we were chosen by God to share his brief but happy life.

Our son taught us many lessons and left us with many joyous memories. With all that he endured, he was a little person who could always clap his hands and smile at life!

May we all follow his wonderful example!

Afterword: A Physician's Perspective

By Leonard L. Bailey, M.D., pediatric cardiac surgeon at Loma Linda University in Loma Linda, California, who headed Nicholas' heart transplant team.

In April a call came to Cheri, the heart transplant coordinator for Loma Linda University Medical Center. It was from the Southern California Regional Organ Procurement Agency, based on the UCLA campus. A little girl who had found and swallowed far too much of her father's sedative medication had been declared brain-dead after attempts to revive her failed. Her brain and brain stem had swollen fiercely, shutting off their blood supply. She was completely dependent upon artificial support systems, which were postponing death of all her other organ systems. Her organs had been donated for purposes of transplantation.

There was no immediate call for liver or kidneys that particular afternoon, but a little girl who lay dying in a hospital in another county, whom we had accepted as a heart transplant recipient, was a good match for the Los Angeles girl's heart. When the news was relayed to the recipient family, however, instead of joy they suddenly felt fear. Somehow they could not bear the reality of having their daughter's heart transplanted. No was the answer. "No, we cannot go through with it!" Their little girl died a few days later.

The Millers had made contact with us after their son had been recommended for a heart transplant by their pediatric cardiologist, Dr. Marvin Auerbach. He had watched fourteen-month-old Nicholas carefully and determined that if the child was to live at all, it would be by means of heart transplantation. His little patient's heart, with no reserve, was acting more like a balloon than a pump. The transplant team had been interviewing the Millers, and an appointment had been scheduled for an outpatient visit with Dr. Eugene Petry, Loma Linda pediatric cardiologist and member of the infant heart transplant team.

Cheri and I sat across the desk from each other, pondering the final decision made by the parents of the little girl dying of heart disease fifty minutes away near the beach cities of southern California. The donor heart, we knew, was also a good match for Nicholas, but he had not yet been formally registered as a heart transplant recipient with the organ procurement agency. Should we let this precious donor heart go, or should we offer it to the Millers? After all, donor organs in this age group were exceedingly difficult to come by. Cheri contacted the donor infant's hospital and the procurement agency. Clearly we had only a few more hours to make alternate plans, and I got on the telephone to Nicholas' cardiologist and ultimately to Jayne, who was working that Friday evening. She sounded stunned by the urgency, but what I soon came to know as her very characteristic self-assurance and courage were quite evident in our conversation. She and Tom had to make one of the most difficult decisions of their lives practically on the spot and get back to us that evening.

"Dr. Bailey," said Jayne on the other end of the telephone connection an hour later, "we've got to talk about it. We're coming down." I met the Millers about midnight that night and could not help but see Nancy, my wife, and myself in Jayne and Tom's shoes as we discussed together the many known and unknown details of heart transplantation for Nicholas. This was, after all, very new territory. We had been studying the application of heart transplantation to newborns and young infants for a number years in the surgical research laboratories of Loma Linda University. After experience with over 150 newborn heart transplants in laboratory animals, our first venture into newborn heart transplantation was met with vigorous international debate and mixed public and professional reviews. Baby Fae had lived twenty days longer than nature had intended after a monkey heart had been used to replace her own severely malformed heart. Hers was not a perfect score for infant heart transplantation, but her experience set the stage for options. One year later, a random newborn heart donor referral was received by Cheri at exactly the time when a four-day-old boy was dying in our Medical Center of hypoplastic left heart disease. Known as Baby Moses, he became the youngest organ recipient in history. Then came Baby Eve, whose donor heart was found by national computer networks. Now equipped with this very limited but unique experience, we were faced with Nicholas. He represented yet a new challenge, because at fourteen months his immune system should react much the same as an adult's system would respond to transplanted tissue. We were encouraged by Drs. Denton Cooley and Bud Frazier's successful heart transplant in an eight-month-old baby a year earlier at Texas Heart Institute.

Now, as I stood opposite these two frightened adoptive parents, I felt very much a part of them and their experience. "We can't let an adopted baby die," I remember saying to them while thinking of my own two adopted sons. I wanted to sound reassuring both to them and to myself. The next morning, my professional colleagues and I replaced Nicholas' terribly damaged heart with a perfect new one. "What a difference," I thought during next morning's rounds. "What a difference a day makes." Nicholas had sailed through surgery without a hitch. Jayne and Tom were ecstatic, and the next two and one-half weeks, I suspect, were among the happiest they had ever spent with their son.

Nicholas was beautiful and absolutely compelling the day he was discharged. His parents were unbelievably happy. They had quickly become a very real part of Loma Linda's small transplant family. Nicholas had had a heart biopsy before being discharged; there was no rejection. He would be followed regularly as an outpatient by members of our developing infant heart transplant team, but perhaps the most intense responsibility lay on Tom and Jayne's shoulders. Their experience during the next months was, I believe, very intense. Tom tried to commute to his job in the Bay Area and Jayne was adapting to life in a small apartment in the nearby town of Colton.

About five weeks after Nicholas was discharged, his testing data suggested the onset of a severe rejection episode, and he was readmitted for observation and increased doses of antirejection medication. His rejection response was undaunted, however. After an acute onset of blockage of the electrical conduction system of his heart, which required emergency placement of a temporary pacemaker, he was placed on a ten-day course of a special antibody preparation called antithymocyte globulin. This drug broke the rejection response. His abnormal test results began gradually to revert to normal, and he was again discharged. I had witnessed this rejection response many times in our experimental animals, but I was unprepared for the awesome chill I experienced when faced with this reality in a much-loved baby boy. I was scared and couldn't show it. Our whole team was scared and not a little tense. Fright was written all over Tom and Jayne's faces. The only cool cucumber was Nicholas, who, though not feeling well and breathing rapidly, perceived little of the danger and did all he could to comfort everyone with his astonishing eyes and smile. This time he was once again a winner.

After Nicholas' second discharge from the Medical Center, life seemed to develop some routine for the Millers. They relocated to the mountain community of Blue Jay, near Lake Arrowhead, about a forty minutes' drive from the University Medical Center. There they began to write this account of their rollercoaster life with Nicholas, every moment of which they cherished. Jayne was helping us devise educational materials for parents of transplanted infants and working with other families with similar experiences. They became an integral part of Loma Linda life and graced it well with courage, humor, and endurance.

Then one day late in August, Jayne called to tell of her concern about Nicholas. He had been seen earlier that week as an outpatient and everything had checked out okay. But for two days now he had vomited and seemed off-color. It was Saturday morning, and Cheri suggested that Jayne bring Nicholas down the mountain to be admitted for observation. No one really wanted this, least of all Nicholas, whose only physical sign of trouble was a slightly fast breathing rate. His activity level was not unusual, but his appetite was off. He vomited again in the hospital. Preliminary testing again showed signs of rejection—a marked change from his evaluation earlier in the week. A plastic catheter was placed in one of his veins, and large doses of antirejection drugs were begun. There was no perceptible change in his condition on Saturday. By Sunday morning, however, both Tom and Jayne saw their son's condition deteriorate. His typically warm extremities had grown cool, his respirations were more rapid, and he was listless. Antithymocyte globulin was once again initiated by vein, but to no avail. Within a couple of hours, to our horror, we all watched Nicholas as he rapidly deteriorated. A tube was placed into his windpipe so that a mechanical ventilator could help his breathing. He became limp and cold. His skin became gray and mottled. Heart-supportive drugs were ineffective. Harsh reality chilled us to the bone. Nicholas was dying, and nothing we tried was making a difference. A part of each of us was dying with him.

Cheri frantically registered him for a replacement heart, but it was a futile effort. The respiratory therapist was by now using a hand bag to breathe for Nicholas, and I was performing heart massage. Several hours went by. We were all drenched in perspiration. Tom and Jayne spent the last hour with us and with their son, doing their best to "will" life into him. At the same time, they were clearly coming to grips with reality. "He just isn't going to survive," I said to the Millers, who like the rest of us were frustrated and completely exhausted. No doubt they had already come to that conclusion. "I think we should stop, don't you?" I asked. "We have no choice, then?" Tom asked, rhetorically and in utter defeat.

We each expressed sorrow to one another in a variety of ways. Nicholas was given a small dose of morphine, the tube was removed from his airway, and heart massage was stopped. As his mother held him, what little life remained in Nicholas ebbed away. The mechanical sounds in the room faded, giving way to painful emotion and finally to quiet heartbreak.

This book is a reminder in very poignant terms of what it means to love someone, to give all you can and more, to cope with risks as big as life and death, and to be much better for having someone touch down in your life, if only for a brief time. The Millers exemplify humanity in its best form. They have enriched my life more than I can say; and now that you've shared in the joy of Nicholas, I think you'll be richer, too.

Acknowledgments

When this book was begun, we were living in Blue Jay and anticipated a far different ending. Nicholas was then recovering rapidly from his transplant surgery—progressing by leaps and bounds. The story was to have ended with our seeing Nicholas immediately after surgery. Then there was to have been a brief epilogue brimming with hope and bringing the reader up to date. In light of real events, that the book has been completed at all is more a tribute to the persuasiveness and encouragement of our family, friends, and colleagues than it is to ourselves. Once persuaded, we tried to function as professionals. It was no easy task.

As the events in this story unfolded, we were helped and encouraged by many dozens of kind and thoughtful people. To all those who gave of themselves, we extend our gratitude. In particular we would like to say thank you to Patricia Ciucci, who provided love and a word processor when we were living out of suitcases; Eli Hall for his criticisms and useful revision suggestions; Jane Hall for allowing us to take over her "Indian Room"; John Thomas, Barbara Taylor, Jan Needham, Kathleen Bennett, Maureen Buckley and Steve Albertolle, Fr. Leo McCaffrey, Nan Trowbridge, Fr. Thomas Murray, and Tom McMahon for spearheading the relief that kept us going; Rebecca Laird, our editor, who guided all our efforts; and Clayton Carlson, publisher of Harper & Row, San Francisco, who believed in our story and had faith in our ability to write it.